Also by Michael Price
From Indigo Sea Press

How to Manage Money Like a Minister

Murder on the Disoriented Express

indigoseapress.com

Backfill

How the Later Gospel Writers
Transformed the Historical Jesus
Into the Risen Christ

By

Michael Price

Clear Light Books
Published by Indigo Sea Press
Winston-Salem

Clear Light Books
Indigo Sea Press
PO Box 26701
Winston-Salem, NC 27114

The opinions, observations, insights and scholarship expressed in this book are purely the work of the author and not of the publisher or any other involved in the publication of this book.

Copyright 2020 by Michael Price
All rights reserved, including the right of reproduction in whole or part in any format.
First Clear Light Books edition published
November, 2020
Clear Light Books, Moon Sailor and all production design are trademarks of Indigo Sea Press, used under license.

For information regarding bulk purchases of this book, digital purchase and special discounts, please contact the publisher at indigoseapress@gmail.com

Cover Concept by Michael Price
Cover design by Pan Morelli
Manufactured in the United States of America
ISBN 978-1-63066-507-4

Dedication

Have you ever noticed how one thing leads to another? We strike up a conversation with a person on an elevator, and the conversation leads to a new job with higher pay...a wrong turn leads to the discovery of a house for sale that's exactly what we're looking for...a first-time guest in worship has their choice of places to sit but chooses to sit in the same pew as you and thus begins a friendship that will last decades. Herein lies the premise of how this work came to maturity.

To the best of my recollection, it was in the early fall of 2006, and I was returning home to Washington, NC, after making a hospital call in nearby Greenville. Suddenly, a sign catches my eye advertising that not only was a satellite campus for Mt. Olive College (now the University of Mt. Olive) under construction, but the school was enrolling new students. On a whim, I stopped, introduced myself to the receptionist, and asked if the campus was looking to hire adjunct instructors. The next thing I knew I was sitting in the office of the site director at the time, Dr. Evan Duff, talking about my credentials to teach, including my undergraduate degree in history, a MA in American History, a Master of Divinity degree, along with a doctorate from George Washington University. The rest is history!

But that serendipitous event was only the beginning, because during the next eight years, I had the honor of teaching classes in American History, Historical Geography, Old and New Testament, and World and Near East Religions in several sites in eastern North Carolina...and not just with the University of Mt. Olive...but with North Carolina Wesleyan College.

In one sense, it is to Dr. Duff, along with his successor at UMO, Lita Ward, and Joy Smallwood at NCWC, that this book is somewhat dedicated. These three individuals allowed me an opportunity to do something that I had only dreamed about doing, namely, teaching at the college level.

Similarly, this book is dedicated to all those hundreds of students…traditional and non-traditional…that I had the honor of teaching during those eight-years. These students, many of whom had full-time jobs during the day and family responsibilities awaiting them at home following class, demonstrated to me the depth and degree of their commitment to learning. Although many were dead-tired from their day jobs, these dedicated students came to class with open minds. It was clear they were not only willing to put in the time and effort but were ready to devote themselves to learning the subject. Beyond inspiring me to be a better instructor, their questions on matters of history and religion, especially the Bible, required that I be ready to answer their probing questions of who and why each class session. It was these students, particularly those in the Survey of the New Testament classes, that had a hand in birthing the idea of writing a book that explores the countless inconsistencies, discrepancies, and alternate facts found in the gospels of Matthew, Luke, and John. More, it was the questions raised by the students following an end-of-class exercise in which they were asked to compare and contrast the Easter story using the four gospels that set me on a path to find out how the later gospel writers went about transforming the historical Jesus into the Risen Christ.

In like manner, this book is dedicated to the history professors at West Liberty State College (now University) and West Virginia University that taught me the value of historical research, the professors at Brite Divinity School (Texas Christian University) who first introduced me to the historical-critical approach to understanding the Bible, and the professors at George Washington University. They taught me how to put all of my learning into written form. Combined, these gifted and patient professors had a hand in transforming me from an individual that accepted things as they were presented to one that felt challenged to look behind every word, every phrase, and every paragraph with reservation and question.

A personal note of thanks also goes out to those individuals that took the time to proof this work and offer me their honest opinions, including, Caren Avera and Bill Northrop. Your keen attention to detail and respect for the English language made me a better author. As well, my personal gratitude is extended to the wonderful folks at Indigo Sea Press and Mike Simpson for the opportunity to publish a third book under their impeccable guidance. They were not only professional and constructive, but they treated me as if I were their only writer.

Above all, this book is dedicated to my loving wife, Betty, who also had the honor of teaching at UMO. Many a day, I would leave her alone at home as I went to the library to prepare to teach my evening classes. For over a decade, she was willing to sacrifice our time together so that I could pursue a dream. Even now, during those yearly trips to Martha's Vineyard and those weekly trips to Ft. De Soto beach, she has been the consummate wife, understanding mate, and dedicated partner. My prayer is that she will come to realize just how much she is a part of this work even as her declining memory continues to overtake her once brilliant mind.

Introduction

"Retirement is the beginning of the time when you can sit back and give advice to others, even though you never followed it in your own life." (Unknown)

As I write this book, I have begun receiving pension checks from my denomination's pension fund. After nearly thirty-five years in parish ministry...seven different churches...in four different states...and two denominations, I feel I have irrevocably escaped the earthly bounds. No longer do I sense the denominational restraints of having to watch what I say for fear of losing my ministerial standing or any future positions. Likewise, gone are the congregational restrictions that are placed on someone in my position as a preacher. The fear of losing a paycheck, while at the same time jeopardizing my livelihood from something I've said from the pulpit, were sometimes theologically paralyzing. But now, I'm retired! Subsequently, I am no longer chained to a set of ecclesiastical or denominational dogma.

> *...today, the gloves come off!*

In the words of the late Dr. Martin Luther King, Jr., "free at last, free at last. Thank God Almighty, I'm free at last."

Most importantly, I have sensed in this newly discovered freedom a calling to write on a subject that has been heavy on my heart for some time; namely, the process by which the later gospel writers known today as Matthew, Luke, and John, went about transforming an itinerate preacher named Jesus into the Risen Christ. In what may be termed an op-ed in book form, the words on the pages that follow are without reserve. While I grudgingly acknowledge that there was once a fear to share such feelings during my pre-retirement years, today, the gloves come off!

Granted, I am not an expert in any field, let alone biblical history and the textual critical approach to understanding anything found in the Bible. I will leave that to the scholars who were doing their own thing for the past thirty-five years while I was writing sermons, calling on my members, and attending committee meetings. Who knows where I might be today if I had enrolled in a Greek or Hebrew class in seminary? Rather than this being my third book, it may well have been my twenty-third. Consequently, this work will not be for everyone.

Naturally, this work is not for scholars. There will be no new manuscripts presented that were recently uncovered by an aspiring graduate student as they were researching in the musty basement of an old library in some remote monastery. Subsequently, this work will produce no new findings that set the academic world ablaze. Noticeably absent from this work will also be a long list of citations that are common among scholarly works, any semblance of this work being peer-reviewed, and no "if you want to know more, then go here." Citing page after page of references would only add unnecessary length to this work, and, in turn, increase the cost of this book. Outside of the apparent reason that this particular work could provide scholars with yet another angle to explain how the gospel writers went about transforming the historical Jesus into the Risen Christ, the only other real purpose for scholars to be interested in the pages of this work is to supply them with some added protection to line the bottom of their birdcages.

In scholarly fashion, let me state without hesitation or reserve that this work is solely my work, and my only primary source of information is the Bible (NRSV), and the four gospels of the New Testament. The contents of this work will not use any book, letter, or epistle of the New Testament beyond the four gospels, and this includes nothing from (Luke) Acts and nothing from Paul's writings since he is more of a "post-resurrection" guy. If the thoughts and conclusions are found to parallel with another writer's work, it is strictly by

> *I taught at the college level, but that does not make me a scholar, or this work scholarly, in any sense of the word.*

chance. Since this work is an original one and meant to stand alone on the research and the merits of this writer, I did not rely on the filters of others telling me what a particular passage may or may not mean. I taught at the college level, yes, but that does not make me a scholar, or this work scholarly, in any sense of the word. I will be the first to admit that the contents which follow are simplistic and light-years away from being of academic caliber...technically, grammatically, or otherwise.

Scholarship aside, this work is written by a novice and directed at all those novices, be they Christian or non-Christian, who are confused by all those inconsistencies, inaccuracies, and contradictions about Jesus in the gospels. This work is an all-out effort by someone aware of the confusion that readers are getting as they read the gospels and wants to assist them in their understanding.

Whatever might be drawn from my words, I am not trying to offend anyone, be they scholar, Sunday School teacher, or student. Neither am I attempting to discredit any professors that I had in seminary nor burn any bridges with former church members or friends. And although

> *I have allowed the facts to lead me to certain conclusions and not the other way around.*

many will find this work objectionable, even distasteful, since it does nothing but deviate from what most know today as orthodox Christianity, I have allowed the facts to lead me to certain conclusions and not the other way around. Simply stated, this book seeks to demonstrate how the later gospel writers we know today as Matthew, Luke, and John utilized the elements of *chronology*, *context*, and *cause* to transform Jesus' life, ministry, and resurrection as found in Mark's gospel into a gospel that was more in-line with their theology of Jesus. Further, this work will show that in certain instances, these three writers took certain events, people, and places found in Mark's gospel, massaged them, and then systematically reconstructed Mark's version of Jesus' life using their own words whenever they felt the need. Rather than work from front to back, birth to resurrection, and simply record what they came to know about Jesus of Nazareth in an upfront and unbiased approach, Matthew, Luke, and John did just the opposite. They intentionally and deliberately reconstructed the life of Jesus. Henceforth, I have come to refer to their practice as backfilling…a construction term whereby builders place dirt behind a newly constructed or existing wall or structure.

And while we're talking about structure and support, here's the structure and the support of how I will go about advancing the belief that Matthew, Luke, and John, intentionally crafted a specific theology that depicted the life and times of Jesus as they perceived it.

Because this work involves a broad understanding of the four gospels, we need to begin in the beginning. Henceforth, **Chapter 1** commences with a brief overview of the four gospels, because such an understanding is critical in our quest to recognize how the later writers went about transforming the historical Jesus into the Risen Christ. This general survey of the four gospels will pay special attention to content and organization. Many may choose to "skip" this first section since a great deal of the chapter will be nothing but a review of what they've been hearing for years via sermons and Sunday School lessons. Others may choose to quickly "skim" through the pages as a kind of refresher to things. Still, others will want to "settle down" and spend a little extra time reading the contents of the first chapter, because they know that this will help them to comprehend better the valuable subject matter of the pages that follow. So that the reader understands the contents of this and all other chapters, I conclude each chapter with a summary.

The first several pages of **Chapter 2** will seek to define in general terms the word "backfill" from a construction sense. However, it will be crucial here to remember that I am neither a builder of new homes nor a remodeler of older ones. Subsequently, my knowledge and use of appropriate verbiage will be rudimentary and could well be termed "highly suspect." As we progress through the chapter, the work will turn its focus on more specifics such as why backfill is essential when building, what elements go into producing suitable backfill, etc., since the concept of backfill is pivotal to understanding its role to the thesis of this work. In addition, Chapter 2 will highlight several examples of the "adjustments" that Matthew, Luke, and John made along the way to Mark's gospel. These examples will include: (a) the apparent changes such as those found in Jesus' triumphal entry into Jerusalem (Matthew 21:1-11, Luke 19:28-44, and John 12:12-19, (b) the not-so-obvious differences such as what happened to Mary, Joseph, and Jesus immediately following the birth of Jesus (Matthew records that the family heads directly to Egypt to escape Herod's wrath (Mt. 2:13 -23), while Luke writes nothing about a trip to Egypt (Luke 2:39), and (c) the flat-out additions and deletions…aka backfill…of each writer's contribution to the scripture.

The contents of **Chapter 3** will set the reader on a course to a specific understanding of how the gospel writers endeavored to transform the historical Jesus into his divinity by introducing the first of three key elements that the gospel writers used to advance their efforts to transform the historical Jesus to the Risen Christ; specifically, the element of *chronology*.

Chapter 4 will move to the second of these three elements. Here, the work will explore how the writers used their *context* to aid in their efforts to transform the historical Jesus into the Risen Christ.

Naturally, **Chapter 5** will take a look at the last of the three elements…*cause*…and the way that the writers used the growing Jesus movement to promote that the one born in Bethlehem was the true Son of God.

The contents of **Chapter 6** will seek to not only provide some possible reasons why the later gospel writers took the route they did to transform the historical Jesus into the Risen Christ but also the reasons behind their chosen methodology.

In the final section of the book, **Chapter 7**, some final thoughts are offered.

Table of Contents

- Chapter One 1
  - The Gospel According to Mark 2
  - The Gospel According to Matthew 5
  - The Gospel According to Luke 9
  - The Gospel According to John................................. 12
- Chapter Two.. 19
  - Backfill.. 19
- Chapter Three..26
  - Chronology..26
- Chapter Four 35
  - Context..35
- Chapter Five..50
  - Cause...50
- Chapter Six..64
  - Why...64
- Chapter Seven 90

Backfill

Chapter One

"The beginning is the most important part of the work" (Plato, The Republic)

More relevant words could not have been spoken, because an understanding of the terms and events found in the gospels plays an essential role in understanding how the later gospel writers went about transforming the historical Jesus into the Risen Christ. To begin laying out such an argument without any kind of foundation is ludicrous.

This said the next several pages will supply a general idea of the who, what, when, and where of each gospel beginning with the gospel according to Mark and concluding with the gospel of John. In between, we will do the same with the contents of the gospels of Matthew and Luke. The remaining pages of this foundational chapter will examine the commonalities that exist among the four gospels, especially as they relate to parables and miracles. Although this introductory chapter may seem lengthy, its contents are essential as it lays the foundation for the meaningful sections that lie ahead.

> *...be careful not to confuse quantity with quality,...*

The four gospels that lie at the epicenter of this work are positioned at the beginning of the New Testament portion of the Christian Bible. All told the gospels of Matthew, Mark, Luke, and John make up less than 15% of the twenty-seven books that comprise the New Testament. Tallying eighty-nine chapters, some twenty-four hundred verses, and nearly fifty-five thousand words, the size of the four gospels pale in comparison to the two hundred-sixty chapters, almost eight thousand verses, and the virtually one hundred thirty-eight thousand references to people, places, and proclamations found in the New Testament. However, one must be careful not to confuse quantity with quality, because within the contents of the four gospels are the heart-and-soul of the Christian faith! It is commonly believed that not only were all four gospels written in the span of fifty-years…between 65 – 110 CE…but that the writers of these four gospels were anonymous and simply "attached" the names of several of Jesus' original twelve apostles (Matthew, Mark, Luke, and John) to add credibility to their work. Finally, while Matthew's gospel, the first of the four gospels to appear in the order in the New Testament, and John's gospel, which one might say is the most contemporary of the gospels because it was most likely written sometime in the latter years of the first century or in the early years of the second century, form the bookends, Luke's gospel, along with the gospel according to Mark, is found between the gospels of Matthew and John. Subsequently, this might lead one to believe that the gospel of Matthew is the oldest of the writings. Not so! This esteemed honor belongs to the gospel of Mark. And because of this, it's only appropriate then that we begin our exploration of how the later gospel writers (Matthew, Luke, and John) went about transforming the historical Jesus into the Risen Christ with a brief survey of each gospel beginning with the gospel according to Mark.

The Gospel According to Mark

Believed to have been written circa 65 – 75CE in the Greek language, the gospel of Mark begins with the baptism of Jesus in the Jordan River by John the Baptist. Also, the common consensus is that the writing is

…the shortest of the four gospels…

Backfill

directed at those who seem to know the underlying message of Christ's life, ministry, death, and resurrection. It is widely accepted that the gospel was written in Rome around the time of violent persecutions, or shortly after the deaths of several of Jesus' more devoted followers such as Peter and Paul. While Mark's gospel lays claim to being the shortest of the four gospels in chapters (16) and verses (just over 675), the writer not only seeks to bring out the human side of Jesus but seems to be more concerned with what Jesus did than what he said (nearly one-third of the gospel consists of healings and exorcisms). Case in point: the concluding six of the gospel's sixteen chapters take in the last week of Jesus' life and comprise nearly 40% of the gospel. Lastly, it must be noted that in the earlier manuscripts of the New Testament Mark's gospel ends rather suddenly with the words "So they went out and fled from the tomb, for terror and amazement had seized them; and they said nothing to anyone for they were afraid" (16:8). The much longer ending (vs. 9-20) is universally accepted to have been added to give the gospel a more suitable ending benefitting of the joy and celebration of that first Easter morning. A summary of Mark's gospel includes...

Chapter 1	Proclamation of John the Baptist ("Prepare the way..."), baptism of Jesus, the temptation of Jesus, calls first disciples, Jesus heals (man with an unclean spirit, many at Simon's house, leper)
Chapter 2	Jesus heals a paralytic, calls Levi, proclamation about Sabbath ("Sabbath was made for humankind...")
Chapter 3	Jesus heals man with withered hand, appoints 12 apostles, a house divided
Chapter 4	Parables (sower, lamp under a basket, growing seed, mustard seed), Jesus stills a storm

Michael F. Price

Chapter 5	Healing in Gennesaret, restoring of girl's life
Chapter 6	Rejection of Jesus in Nazareth ("Prophets are not without honor…"), sending out mission of the 12, death of John the Baptist, feeding of the 5,000, Jesus walks on water, healing in Gennesaret
Chapter 7	Things that defile, Jesus calls a Syrophoenician woman a dog, cures a deaf man
Chapter 8	Feeding of the 4,000, a blind man cured in Bethsaida, Jesus foretells his death and resurrection
Chapter 9	The Transfiguration, Jesus heals a boy, Jesus tells of his death and resurrection, who's the greatest, exorcist, teaching about salt
Chapter 10	Teaching about divorce, Jesus blesses the little children, teaching regarding rich man, Jesus tells of his death and resurrection, Jesus and the sons of Zebedee, healing of Bartimaeus
Chapter 11	Jesus' entry into Jerusalem, cleanses the temple of moneychangers, curse the fig tree, authority questioned
Chapter 12	Parable of the wicked tenants, paying taxes ("give therefore, to the emperor …"), the great commandment, the widow's gift
Chapter 13	Prediction/destruction of temple, lesson of the fig tree
Chapter 14	Conspiracy against Jesus, anointing at Bethany, Judas agrees to betray Jesus, Passover with disciples, Lord's Supper, Peter's denial, Jesus in Gethsemane, the

Backfill

	arrest of Jesus, trial before the council, Peter's denial
Chapter 15	Jesus before Pilate, Jesus is handed over for crucifixion, death of Jesus on the cross, burial
Chapter 16	The resurrection of Jesus (shorter ending), resurrection (longer ending), Jesus appears before 2 of his disciples, appears to the 11, ascension

The Gospel According to Matthew

It does not take long for one to recognize that some major "adaptations" are beginning to take place between the contents of Mark's gospel and Matthew's understanding of the events surrounding the life and ministry of Jesus. First, one recognizes that Matthew's gospel has increased in length (nearly 75% from that of Mark's gospel), over 50% in total verses, and over 60% in verbiage. Whereas Mark begins his gospel with the baptism of Jesus, Matthew commences his gospel by presenting the genealogy of Jesus, and the proclamation that Jesus is the Messiah. Immediately after that, Matthew follows with an account of Jesus's birth and the visit of the wise men. From there, it becomes apparent that Matthew "borrows" much of his material...upwards of 90%...from Mark's gospel. Composed in Greek and thought to have been written in the last quarter of the first century (circa 75-85CE), Matthew's goal is to present Jesus as the long-awaited Jewish savior (2:2, 21:5, 21:9) to a mainly Jewish Christian community. Subsequently, the writer makes extensive use of Old Testament references while giving the impression that the words came directly from the mouth of Jesus and not from the

>...*Matthew "borrows" much of his material...*

Michael F. Price

pen of Matthew. Still, Matthew is quick to demonstrate that within his writings are several distinct additions that are absent in Mark's gospel, including the events surrounding the Sermon on the Mount (i.e., the Beatitudes, the Lord's Prayer, the Golden Rule, and the Great Commission). Lastly, it seems that Matthew wanted to make his gospel seem more dramatic by including the tearing of the curtain temple, an earthquake, and resurrection of the saints (27:51-ff). A necessary review of the structure and organization of Matthew's gospel takes in…

Chapter 1	The genealogy of Jesus, his birth
Chapter 2	The visit of the Magi, the escape to Egypt, the massacre by Herod, the return from Egypt
Chapter 3	Declaration of John the Baptist, the baptism of Jesus
Chapter 4	The temptation of Jesus, the ministry launched in Galilee, Jesus calls his first disciples
Chapter 5	Sermon on the Mount (the Beatitudes, teachings about anger, adultery, retaliation)
Chapter 6	Sermon on the Mount (proclamations about prayer, Lord's Prayer), serving two masters
Chapter 7	Sermon on the Mount (judging others, ask/seek/knock, Golden Rule, hearers and doers)
Chapter 8	Jesus cleanses a leper, heals Peter's mother-in-law, stills the storm, heals two demoniacs in Gadarene
Chapter 9	Jesus heals a paralytic, calling of Matthew, restoring of girl's life, healing of blind men, healing of mute man, proclamation that the harvest is great but workers few
Chapter 10	Calling/mission of the 12 apostles, coming persecutions, a proclamation that Jesus is not bringing peace but a sword

Backfill

Chapter 11	Message sent to John the Baptist, praises him, message to Chorazin and Bethsaida, come to Him all who are weary and heavy-laden
Chapter 12	Jesus heals the man with a withered hand, tells followers not to tell anyone, a house divided
Chapter 13	Parables (sower, parable explained, mustard seed, yeast), Jesus is rejected in Nazareth (carpenter's son, son of Mary?)
Chapter 14	Death of John the Baptist, feeding of the 5,000, Jesus walks on water, heals in Gennesaret
Chapter 15	Jesus teaching of things that defile, Jesus calls Canaanite woman a dog
Chapter 16	Leaders demand a sign from Jesus, Peter's declaration, Jesus foretells his death and resurrection, conditions of discipleship (take up their cross)
Chapter 17	The Transfiguration of Jesus, a boy is healed, Jesus foretells his death and resurrection
Chapter 18	Differences over greatness, parable of lost sheep, parable of unforgiving servant
Chapter 19	Teaching regarding marriage and divorce, Jesus blesses the little children, teaching regarding rich young man
Chapter 20	Parable (laborers in the vineyard), Jesus foretells his death and resurrection (3), Jesus and the sons of Zebedee
Chapter 21	Jesus' entry into Jerusalem, cleanses the temple of moneychangers, curse the fig tree, authority questioned, parable (two sons, wicked tenants)

Michael F. Price

Chapter 22	Parable of wedding banquet, paying taxes ("give therefore, to the emperor..."), Jesus questioned about the resurrection, greatest commandment)
Chapter 23	Jesus' proclamation against scribes and Pharisees, Jesus laments over Jerusalem
Chapter 24	Prediction/destruction of temple, lesson of the fig tree, parable of the faithful/unfaithful servant
Chapter 25	Parable (10 bridesmaids, talents), last judgement separation of sheep/goats, welcoming strangers
Chapter 26	Conspiracy against Jesus, anointing at Bethany, Judas agrees to betray Jesus, Passover with disciples, Lord's Supper, Peter's denial, Jesus in Gethsemane, arrest of Jesus, trial before Caiaphas, Peter's denial
Chapter 27	Jesus before Pilate, suicide of Judas, Jesus is handed over for crucifixion, death of Jesus on the cross, burial
Chapter 28	The resurrection of Jesus, disciples commissioned ("Go therefore, and make disciples...")

Backfill

The Gospel According to Luke

Commonly believed to have been written to both draw and win over cultured Greeks to the Christian faith, the gospel writer known today as Luke was writing his gospel around the same time as Matthew (circa 75-90CE). But while Luke's gospel is four chapters shorter than his contemporary Matthew, Luke makes up for the difference by including more verses and words in his gospel.

> *...it is apparent that Luke not only seeks "to cut his own path" but...*

In one sense, Luke follows the lead of Matthew and draws a great deal (nearly 60%) of his subject matter from Mark's gospel. Just as his counterpart, Luke includes in his gospel something of the birth narrative (2:1-ff), the genealogy of Jesus (3:23-38), and the Lord's Prayer (11:2-4). However, in what may be called Matthew 2.0, Luke includes a somewhat redacted version of the Sermon on the Mount, which he conveniently terms the Sermon on the Plains (6:17-49). Furthermore, Luke seldom, if ever, uses any citations from the Old Testament to acclaim Jesus as the Chosen One, and commonly employs words that are absent among the remaining pages of the New Testament. Above all, it is apparent that Luke not only seeks to "cut his own path" but also take a jab at other writers with his opening words: "Since many have undertaken to set down an orderly account of events that have been fulfilled among us, just as they were handed on to us by those who from the beginning were eyewitnesses and servants of the word, I too decided, after investigating everything carefully from the very first to write an orderly account..." (1:1-3). Luke's orderly account includes...

Michael F. Price

Chapter 1	Promise of John the Baptist's birth, the Annunciation, Mary visits Elizabeth, the birth of John the Baptist
Chapter 2	Birth of Jesus, visit by angels and shepherds, Presentation in the temple, return to Galilee, Jesus at 12-years
Chapter 3	Proclamation of John the Baptist ("Prepare the way…"), baptism of Jesus, ancestry of Jesus
Chapter 4	The temptation of Jesus, ministry launched in Galilee, rejection of Jesus in Nazareth ("no prophets is accepted…"), heals (man with unclean spirit, Simon's mother-in-law honor…")
Chapter 5	Miraculous catch, Jesus calls his first disciples, Jesus cleanses a leper and a paralytic, calls Levi
Chapter 6	Jesus questioned about the Sabbath, heals man with a withered hand, choosing of 12 apostles, teaching on the plain (love of enemies, judging others, hearers and doers)
Chapter 7	Jesus raises widow's son, John's questions to Jesus, woman with the ointment
Chapter 8	Women following Jesus, parables (sower, lamp under jar), Jesus' relatives, stills the storm, heals demoniac in Gadarene, restoring of girl's life
Chapter 9	Releasing of the 12 apostles, feeding of the 5,000, Peter's declaration, Jesus foretells his death and resurrection (1), The Transfiguration of Jesus, a boy is healed, Jesus foretells his death and resurrection (2), Jesus refused in Samaria, nature of discipleship

Backfill

Chapter 10	Mission of the 70, message to Chorazin and Bethsaida, return of the parable (Good Samaritan), Mary and Martha
Chapter 11	Jesus teaches Lord's Prayer, persistent prayer (ask, search, knock)
Chapter 12	Hypocrisy of Pharisees, courageous confession, parable (rich fool), teaching not to worry, faithful/unfaithful slave, a house divided
Chapter 13	Jesus heals a crippled woman, parables (barren fig tree, mustard seed, yeast, narrow door), grief over Jerusalem
Chapter 14	Jesus heals a man with dropsy, teaching on humility, parable of the great dinner, cost of discipleship ("Whoever does not carry the cross..."), teaching about salt
Chapter 15	Parables (lost sheep, prodigal son)
Chapter 16	Parables (unjust manager, rich man and Lazarus)
Chapter 17	Sayings of Jesus, healing of 10 lepers, coming kingdom
Chapter 18	Parables (widow and unjust judge, Pharisee and tax collector, rich ruler), Jesus blesses the little children, Jesus foretells his death and resurrection, Jesus heals a blind man
Chapter 19	Jesus and Zacchaeus, parable of the 10-pounds, Jesus' entry into Jerusalem, weeping over Jerusalem, cleanses the temple of moneychangers
Chapter 20	Jesus authority questioned, parable of the wicked tenants, questioned paying taxes ("then give to the emperor..."), resurrection

Chapter 21	The widow's gift, foretelling of the destruction of Jerusalem, lesson of the fig tree
Chapter 22	Conspiracy to kill Jesus, Lord's Supper, greatness in the kingdom, Jesus predicts Peter's denial, Jesus prays on the Mount of Olives, Peter denial, trial before the council
Chapter 23	Jesus and Pilate, Jesus and Herod, sentence, crucifixion, death and burial of Jesus
Chapter 24	Resurrection, appearance on the Emmaus road, appears to disciples, ascension

The Gospel According to John

Using simple addition, the total number of chapters of the twenty-seven books of the New Testament equals two hundred sixty. Likewise, the sum of the verses of these twenty-seven writings is nearly eight

> *...John's gospel seems a satisfying compromise*

thousand, while the total number of words of the New Testament are just over one hundred thirty-eight thousand. But if Christians are asked to identify the most recognized verse among the nearly eight thousand verses of the New Testament, the winner would undoubtedly be John 3:16: "For God so loved the world that he gave his only Son, so that everyone who believes in him may not perish but may have eternal life." Such is the impact that the Gospel According to John has made on Christian theology. Commonly believed to have been written in the waning years of the first century or the first decade of the second century (circa 90-110CE), the number of chapters (21), total verses (less than 900), and total words (nearly 16,000) of John's gospel seems a satisfying compromise between that which one finds among the

Backfill

three other gospels. Still, one must not allow these figures to lessen the impact this gospel has made transforming the historical Jesus into the Risen Christ. Beginning with a bold declaration that Jesus is the "Logos"... the Word becoming flesh...it is readily apparent that John has less in common with the writings of Matthew, Mark, and Luke than one might believe. For starters, John seems to be the only one of his counterparts to come right out and call Jesus the Son of God. From there, one finds nothing but affirmations of Jesus' divine role among John's verses, including the countless times Jesus speaks in the first person proclaiming that he is the bread of life (6:35), the resurrection and the life (11:25), and, most notably, that the Father and I (he) are one (10:30). In a further effort to demonstrate the uniqueness of his gospel, John conveniently omits specific episodes that we find in Matthew, Mark, and Luke, including no story of Jesus' baptism, no temptation of Jesus, exorcisms, and no Sermon on the Mount. Instead, John inserts such events as the miracle at the wedding in Cana, where Jesus turns the water into wine, and foot-washing in-place of the circumstances surrounding the Last Supper. A brief outline of John's gospel consists of...

Chapter 1	Word becomes flesh, the witness of John the Baptist, Jesus calls Simon Peter, Andrew, Philip, Nathaniel
Chapter 2	Wedding in Cana (water into wine), cleanses the temple of moneychangers
Chapter 3	Jesus and Nicodemus ("For God so loved the World..."), Jesus and John and the One from Heaven
Chapter 4	Jesus and the Samaritan woman, Jesus goes back to Galilee, Jesus heals in Cana
Chapter 5	Jesus heals on the Sabbath, divine authority of the Son
Chapter 6	Feeding of the 5,000, Jesus walks on

	water, bread from heaven, Jesus calls Judas the devil
Chapter 7	The unbelief of Jesus' brothers, Jesus teaches in the temple, attempt to arrest Jesus, the uncertainty of people regarding Jesus
Chapter 8	Woman caught in adultery, Jesus as the light of the world, Jesus foretells impending death, Abraham and Jesus
Chapter 9	Jesus restores sight to a blind man, healing on the Sabbath, spiritual blindness
Chapter 10	Jesus as the Good Shepherd, Jews reject Jesus
Chapter 11	Passing of Lazarus, Jesus declaration ("I am the resurrection and the life…"), Jesus criticized, Lazarus raised from the dead, conspiracy to kill Jesus
Chapter 12	Anointing of Jesus by Mary, Jesus' entry into Jerusalem, Jesus proclamation about his death, summation of Jesus' teachings ("…for I came not to judge the world…")
Chapter 13	Jesus' foot-washing, Jesus talks about betrayal by Judas, new commandment ("…love one another…"), Jesus predicts Peter's denial
Chapter 14	Jesus and doubting Thomas, the promise of the Holy Spirit
Chapter 15	Jesus as the True Vine ("I am the true vine and my Father is the Vine grower…")
Chapter 16	Jesus' future peace for the disciples
Chapter 17	Jesus prays for his disciples
Chapter 18	Arrest of Jesus, Jesus before the high priest, Peter's denial, Jesus questioned by Caiaphas, Peter's second denial, Jesus before Pilate, Jesus sentenced
Chapter 19	Sentence reconsidered by Pilate, the

Backfill

	decision to crucify, last words, death, and burial of Jesus
Chapter 20	Resurrection, appearance to Mary Magdalene, the other disciples, Thomas, the purpose of this book
Chapter 21	Jesus appears before seven disciples, Jesus talks with Peter ("...feed my sheep..."), much more that could not be written

Summary: From the preceding few pages, it is apparent that there exists a host of commonalities among the gospels, including such elements as people, places, and parables. A more comprehensive and in-depth reading of the material found in the gospels reveals even more noteworthiness among the pages. Consider the following...

Of the 40-plus parables that appear in the synoptic gospels (Matthew, Mark, and Luke), thirty-one appear in the gospel of Luke, twenty-three within the gospel of Matthew. Nine are among the pages of Mark's gospel. Among these eight shared parables are the parable of the mustard seed (Matthew 13:31-32, Mark 4:30-32, Luke 13:18-19), the parable of the wicked tenants (Matthew 21:33-44, Mark 12:1-11, Luke 20:9-18), and the parable of the fig tree (Matthew 24:32-33, Mark 13:28-29, Luke 21:29-31).

> **By definition, there are no parables in the Johannine gospel.**

Of the 35-or-so miracles that appear among the pages of the four gospels, nearly one-third (10) appears in all three synoptic gospels. Among the list are the healing of Peter's mother-in-law (Matthew 8:14-15, Mark 1:30-31, Luke 4:38-39), the resuscitation of Jarius' daughter (Matthew 9:18-25, Mark 5:22-42, Luke 8:41-56), and the Transfiguration (Matthew 17:1-8, Mark 9:2-8, and Luke 9:28-36). Moreover, one finds that sixteen of the miracles found in Matthew's gospel are "borrowed" from Mark's gospel, as are eleven of the miracle stories in Luke, while only two miracles appear in both Mark and John's gospels (John 6:5-13, 6:19-21).

On closer examination, ten parables are unique to the gospel of Matthew, including the parable of the wedding banquet (Matthew 22:2-14) and the parable of the treasure hidden in the field (Matthew 13:44-46). The list of the seventeen parables found solely within the gospel of Luke includes the parable of the lost coin (Luke 15:8-10) and the parable of the prodigal son (Luke 15:11-32). The parable of the secret growing seed (Mark 4:26-29) is the only Markan parable that does not appear in either Matthew or Luke. By definition, there are no parables in the Johannine gospel.

In like manner, there are several miracles found in only one gospel, including the healing of the mute demoniac (Matthew 9:32-33), the blind man at Bethsaida (Mark 8:22-26), the ten lepers (Luke 17:11-19), and the invalid at the pool of Bethsaida (John 5:1-9).

Finally, it appears that there is only one miracle found in all four gospels…the feeding of the 5,000 (Matthew 14:15-21, Mark 6:35-44, Luke 9:12-17, John 6:5-13). Curiously, and true to form, there is a divergence of the facts within the story. While the initial points are in agreement; namely, a huge crowd gathers to hear Jesus speak. But when the group becomes hungry, and there are only five loaves of bread and two fish to be found, what happens after that can only be termed "alternate facts." Matthew (14:13-21) records that when evening had come, and the crowd had become hungry, the disciples recommend that Jesus send the people to a nearby town so they (the members of the crowd) can buy food for themselves. When Jesus tells the disciples to give the crowd something to eat, they (the disciples) reply by saying there's not enough food (only five loaves and two fish). After ordering the crowd to sit down, Jesus takes the loaves and the fish, blesses the food, and promptly orders his disciples to distribute the food. The leftovers were enough to fill twelve baskets. Those that ate were 5,000 men besides women and children. In Mark's gospel (6:31-44), there is mention of the cost to buy food for the group (two hundred denarii), Jesus commanding the crowds sit in groups of hundreds and fifties, and the total being served comprised of men only. Not to be outdone, Luke (9:10-17) takes several of Matthew and Mark's main points such as the plea from the disciples for Jesus to run the crowd off so they will be forced to fend for themselves, the appeal from Jesus for the 5,000 men to divide into groups of fifty, and the 12 baskets of leftovers, but adds the name of a nearby city…Bethsaida…to lend a degree of geographical authenticity to his version. In what seems to be yet another case of "I can do one better," the Johannine author adds more specificity to his understanding of the feeding of the 5,000 by mentioning the Sea of Galilee (aka…Sea of Tiberias), an indication of the time of year this epic event takes place (near the Jewish festival of Passover), the names of two of the disciples that were present that day (Philip and Andrew, the brother of Simon Peter) and the presence of a certain boy, the anticipated cost to purchase enough food for the crowd (two hundred denarii), along with the fact that the loaves were not just any loaves but barley loaves (6:1-14)!

> …*the gospel writers were intentional in their efforts*…

If nothing else, the differences, discrepancies, and inconsistencies found among the parables and the miracles within the gospels lend credence to the focus of this work that the gospel writers were intentional in their efforts to present a "different" Jesus that arose from the grave than the one that was entombed days prior. But before we begin to demonstrate how each gospel writer went about capitalizing on the elements of *chronology*, *context*, and *cause* to advance their particular effort at transforming the historical Jesus into the Risen Christ, we both must define and understand the contemporary concept utilized by the gospel writers to advance their unique theology. The relevant term being *backfill*.

Chapter Two

Backfill

Backfill: to refill (something, such as an excavation) usually with excavated material   (Merriam-Webster Dictionary)

As often as I visit family in West Virginia, the conversations around the dinner table invariably settle on my mechanical ineptitude. One story that always seems to surface is the one in which one of my brothers tells me to go to the toolbox and bring back a left-handed screwdriver. Consequently, it should come as no surprise that when I began my research on this book entitled appropriately enough...*Backfill: How the Later Gospel Writers Transformed the Historical Jesus into the Risen Christ*, I engaged the person that I considered to be the most wisdom-filled person I know in construction-related matters...David Weatherly. The depth and degree of David's knowledge stem from his long years of not only building new homes but re-building and remodeling older ones in eastern North Carolina. If anyone knew about backfill, it would be him. And it was during those countless conversations in person and on the phone that I learned most of the essentials of this construction technique and the specific process involved in backfilling.

> ***...the specific process involved in backfilling.***

The first phase involves clearing the ground around the construction site of debris, including all trees, tree limbs, bushes, grass, and loose stones. If one discovers water during

Michael F. Price

this initial stage, the water must be completely drained, and the ground allowed ample time to dry. During the second phase, a large portion of the dirt removed from the work area is placed nearby, because most builders will reuse much of the same soil that's been removed to later refill the excavated area. The third phase in the process involves the construction of the retaining wall *beginning from the perimeter and working toward the middle*. This step provides valuable lateral support to the structure. Upon completion of the support wall, the subsequent portion of the backfill process begins in earnest as much of the *existing the material* (replacement dirt or similar substance) is piled up against the wall. It is common knowledge in this fourth phase that the *smaller the size of the replacement aggregate means a greater chance of a higher quality backfill*. For example, sand is believed to be better backfill material than mere rubble or chunks of other solid materials.

Similarly, the backfill must be done in *layers, packing, and filling* in all the open spaces as one goes. If done correctly and with attention to detail, the packing of the backfill will reduce the chances of having a weakened foundation and increase the integrity of the structure with a more reliable and stable foundation. Once the backfill is allowed to cure, the fifth and final phase involves the fill dirt being seeded or sodded to *blend in with the surrounding areas*.

Against this backdrop are the numerous ways, apparent and not-so-apparent, that the later gospel writers (Matthew, Luke, and John) went about backfilling the contents of Mark's gospel to advance their efforts at transforming the historical Jesus into the Risen Christ. Consider these points...

> *Nowhere is this "reverse engineering" more prevalent than in the Gospel According to Matthew.*

First, one could state that the

Backfill

possible approach of the later gospel writers of advancing a new perspective of Jesus shows signs that the writers *began in the perimeter* of Jesus' life...aka, his resurrection...and continued inward toward the specifics. Nowhere is this "reverse engineering" more prevalent than in the Gospel According to Matthew.

Not long before Jesus is taken down from the cross, Matthew records that Jesus supposedly utters "...Eli, Eli, lama sabachthani" ("My God, my God, why have you forsaken me?" (27:46). One will discover that these are the exact words found in the opening lines of Psalm 22: "My God, my God, why have you forsaken me" (22:1). As Jesus makes his triumphal entry into Jerusalem, Matthew relates two sayings that seem to have roots in the Old Testament, including Matthew 21:16 (compare Psalm 8:2: "...Out of the mouths of babes and infants..."), and Matthew 21:5 (compare Zechariah 9:9: "...Lo, your king comes to you; triumphant and victorious he is, humble and riding on a donkey."). As one continues to retreat through Matthew's gospel, one finds no less than fifteen references to Jesus as either the Son of David (20:30, 15:22, 12:23, 9:27) or the Son of Man (17:12, 13:37, 12:8). Additionally, one finds a handful of possible references to Hosea (Matthew 2:15 vs. Hosea 11:1), Isaiah (Matthew 3:3 vs. Isaiah 40:3), and Micah (Matthew 2:5-6 vs. Micah 5:2) scattered throughout Matthew's gospel. And in one initial feat to kick-off his effort to backfill the life of Jesus *beginning on the perimeter and working inward*, Matthew begins his gospel listing the genealogy of Jesus...all seventy-plus generations, "...from Abraham...to the Messiah" (1:17). Matthew's efforts to prove to his Jewish audience that Jesus is the Messiah promised via the scriptures are clear and well-crafted. If one needs additional proof, consider these subtle points of commonality: (a) Moses survives Pharaoh's order to kill infants while Jesus survives Herod's efforts to do the same centuries later; (b) Moses all but ends his leadership within sight of the Jordan River while Jesus seemingly begins his ministry as he is baptized in the waters of the Jordan River; and (c) just as Moses is called to lead the twelve tribes, Jesus chooses twelve followers to lead. Clearly, Matthew is "playing to his (Jewish) base" as he endeavors to transform the historical Jesus into the Risen Christ by employing phrases such as "This was to fulfill what had been spoken by the Lord through the prophet" (2:15), "...This is the one of whom the prophet Isaiah spoke..." (3:3), and "...indeed fulfilled the prophecy of Isaiah..." (13:14). More, Matthew succeeds in furthering his case that Jesus is the one sent from God. Matthew is so successful in proving his point that the editors of the New Testament have placed his gospel as the first of the four gospels as it stands as a proper connect from the Old Testament to the New Testament.

In like manner, one can also say that the later gospel writers *utilized much of the existing material* found in Mark's gospel to backfill their gospel. For this, one needs to go no further than remembering the well-established fact that the vast majority of the material found in Mark's gospel is also found among the pages of Matthew and Luke's gospels.

> *...the vast majority of the material found in Mark's gospel is also found among the pages of Matthew and Luke's gospels.*

In more realistic terms, the commonly held understanding is that upwards of ninety percent of Matthew's gospel has parallels with the contents of Mark's gospel. Similarly, Luke's gospel contains over one-half of the material found in Mark. While the vocabulary, events, and sequence of those elements are many times shared, the commonalities communicate a definite sharing of content (Mark 1:21-28 and Luke 4:32-37, Mark 12:41-44 and Luke 21:1-4). Similarly, there are only two events of Mark's gospel found in John's writing (Mark 6:35-44 and John 6:5-13, Mark 6:48-51 and John 6:19-21); however, they are not as numerous as those

Backfill

found in Matthew and Luke. Whatever the case, it becomes clear that the later gospel writers seem to have made use, sometimes quite liberally, of Mark's material in their offerings.

A third example of the elements of backfill that the later gospel writers employed was the *inclusion of small pieces of refill to create a better quality backfill*. Generally speaking, the list includes several passages found in Matthew's gospel which embraces, but is not limited to, the star over Bethlehem (Matthew 2:2), Jesus' healing of two blind men (9:27-31), and the miracle of the coin in the fish's mouth (17:24-27). Likewise, Luke's gospel includes the circumcision of Jesus (2:21), the story of Zacchaeus (19:1-10), and the Emmaus road experience (24:13-ff). Lastly, John's inclusion of *small pieces of refill* to Mark's gospel incorporates the story of the woman at the well (4:4-ff), the healing of the blind man (9:1-12), and the promise of the paraclete (16:5-15).

> *By most standards, this approach of packing is never more apparent than in the Gospel According to John.*

Just as *packing the material* with old and new refill during the backfill process is crucial in making a stable structure, it is clear that the later gospel writers seemingly employed this same tactic to make their particular gospel more enduring. By most standards, this approach of packing is never more apparent than in the Gospel According to John and the nine "I am" statements. Beginning with chapter six and continuing for the next several chapters, John seeks to increase the legitimacy of Jesus' divine claim of God incarnate with a series of self-proclamations. In the first instance, Jesus states that he is the bread of life, and whoever follows him will neither be hungry or thirsty (6:35, 48, 51). Jesus then follows this initial statement with two similar declarations that he is the light of the world (8:12, 9:5). Other announcements include that he is the entrance to eternal life (10:7, 9), the good shepherd (10:11, 14), the resurrection and the life (11:25), the way (14:6), the true vine (15:1, 5), and the "I am he" testimony Jesus spoke to those that came to arrest him (18:5-6). However, the most impactful of the "I am" pronouncements could well be the one found in chapter eight in which Jesus says just before he is stoned by an angry mob that "...before Abraham was, I am." (8:58). With such an expression, John not only succeeds in packing his gospel with lines that Jesus not only existed before the calling of the Jewish patriarch, Abraham, but also that Jesus has always been the pre-existent Son of God...the Logos (1:1-ff).

Last but not least, the later gospel writers seem to finish off their use of backfill by first *allowing the backfill to cure* and then *blend in their words* with the words of Mark. All told, there are as many as twelve common stories found in all four gospels, including the ministry of John the Baptist (Matthew 3:1-12, Mark 1:1-8, Luke 3:1-20, and John 1:19-34), the baptism of Jesus (Matthew 3:13-17, Mark 1:9-11, Luke 3:21-22, and John 1:29-39), the calling of the first disciples (Matthew 4:18-22, Mark 1:16-20, Luke 5:1-11, and John 1:35-51), and the gathering around the Last Supper (Matthew 26:26-29, Mark 14:18-21, Luke 22:17-20, and John 13:1-31). Nevertheless, there is a heavy presence of embellishment among the later writers in these stories as to the sequence and order of events, people involved, and names of places.

Summary: There are countless examples among the words of the later gospel writers of the presence of backfill. Generally speaking, one finds the presence of "reverse-engineering" and working from the perimeter inward within Matthew's gospel that in Jesus one finds the

> *...there is overwhelming proof that the later gospel writers endeavored to blend in their words with the words of Mark.*

Backfill

long-awaited Messiah along with the conviction that his gospel is a continuation of the beliefs outlined in the literature of the Old Testament. One finds no less than two dozen references to either Old Testament passages, prophets of the Old Testament, Jesus as the Son of David, or the Son of Man among Matthew's words. Similarly, one also can find an element of the presence of backfill amid the sentences of Luke's gospel as he attempts to promote his belief of the divinity of Jesus by utilizing a great deal of Mark's gospel when Luke finds it to his benefit. In like manner, one could easily say that within John's gospel there is a pattern of packing taking place in that whenever possible John has Jesus declaring that he (Jesus) is "the one." Lastly, there is overwhelming proof that the later gospel writers endeavored to blend in their words with the words of Mark. Such a technique not only supplies a certain degree of validity and credibility to their writings but also seeks to give the illusion that the later gospel writers are merely adding detail to Mark's gospel.

With this behind us, we now move to identify the three specific elements the later gospel writers utilized to advance their belief that Jesus was more than an itinerate preacher from a town called Nazareth…he was indeed the Son of God! The three elements being *chronology*, *context*, and *cause*.

Michael F. Price

Chapter Three

Chronology

"...timing is everything"
(unknown)

It's true...timing is everything. Drink a bottle of Mountain Dew at 10:00pm, and there's a good chance a person will be awake hours later. That's what one would call bad timing because it usually produces not-so-good results. Other examples of bad timing include buying a house when a person is unemployed, asking your boss for a raise when the company is on the threshold of bankruptcy, or buying stock when the price of that stock is high. Conversely, there is also good timing when a person is in the right place...at the right time...and does the right thing. Good timing can sometimes turn an everyday event into an event for the ages. And I am convinced that the later gospel writers, particularly Matthew, Luke, and John, intentionally produced their respective gospels at just the right time in history. While these writers did not know how impactful their writings would be in furthering Christianity, they used the element of time to their advantage as they went about backfilling the life, ministry, death, and resurrection of Jesus. It will be the goal of this chapter to demonstrate how the later gospel writers used timing in their efforts to transform the historical Jesus into the Risen Christ.

> *...Matthew, Luke, and John intentionally produced their respective gospels at just the right time in history.*

In the opening pages of Matthew's gospel (1:1-ff), one

Backfill

finds the genealogy of Jesus starting with Abraham and ending with Joseph ("...Joseph the husband of Mary, of whom Jesus was born, who is called the Messiah." 1:17). On the surface, it appears Matthew intends to link Jesus to Abraham, and yet in a seemingly backdoor approach, what Matthew successfully succeeds in doing is establishing his foundational belief that Jesus is the long-awaited Jewish Messiah. After laying out forty-two generations of Joseph's genealogy and who-begat-who, the last line of the passage suddenly includes Mary, the mother of Jesus. One finds a similar thing taking place in Luke's gospel (3:23-ff). While Matthew works oldest to youngest (Abraham to Jesus) in his genealogy, Luke does the opposite. He traces Jesus' genealogy from youngest to oldest beginning with Jesus. Luke traces the genealogy of Jesus to Adam (Luke 3:38). Finally, whereas Matthew lists forty-two generations, Luke lists seventy-six names in Jesus' ancestral tree with Heli as the father of Joseph and not Jacob, as Matthew does in his gospel. Whatever the case, it is evident that these two writers are using the element of time to their advantage. Each writer seems to take full benefit of the years between Jesus' birth and the appearance of their respective gospels to free themselves from being "fact-checked" by relatives of Jesus or anybody else. Again, one must remember that it was nearly seventy-years between the birth of Jesus and the appearance of the gospels of Matthew and Luke.

Equally telling in the efforts of the later gospel writers to backfill the life of the historical Jesus is the way Matthew, Luke, and John intentionally labored at reducing the connection of Jesus to his human (family) side. More than once in his gospel, Mark states that Jesus had not only brothers but also sisters. The brothers are named James, Joses, Judas, and Simon, while the sisters go unnamed (3:31, 6:3). Matthew

> *Yet again, one can see the later gospel writers...utilizing the element of time...*

acknowledges Mark's claim for Jesus having brothers but initially mentions no sisters (Matthew 12:46-50). Several verses later in his gospel, Matthew lists the names of Jesus' brothers. However, Matthew spells one of the brother's name as Joses for Joseph and lists Simon before Judas (13:55). Moreover, Matthew now includes in that same chapter that Jesus does have female siblings (13:56). By the time of Luke's writing (circa 75-90CE), the names of the brothers are nowhere to be found among the pages, and there is no mention whatsoever of Jesus having sisters (Luke 8:19-21). The same goes for John's gospel (John 2:12), which could have been written some two decades after Luke's gospel. Yet again, one can see the later gospel writers, particularly Luke and John, utilizing the element of time to their advantage as they seek to deliberately elevate Jesus to his divinity while continuing to minimize his human side. By no longer mentioning Jesus' family by name, it appears that Luke and John were seeking to avoid any possible challenges in their efforts to transform the historical Jesus into the Risen Christ.

A third example of the way the later gospel writers made optimum use of the element of time to backfill their gospel was to lessen the visibility and importance of the disciples. Historically speaking, Mark is the first of the gospel writers to mention the calling of the twelve, naming them in the following order: Simon (Peter), James and John (sons of Zebedee), Andrew, Philip, Bartholomew, Matthew, Thomas, James (son of Alphaeus), Thaddaeus, Simon (the Cananaean), and Judas Iscariot, "...who betrayed Jesus" (Mark 3:13-19). With minor changes, Matthew lists the order of the calling of the original disciples as Simon (Peter), his brother, Andrew, James and John (sons of Zebedee), Philip, Bartholomew, Thomas, Matthew (the tax collector), James (son of Alphaeus), Thaddaeus, Simon (the Cananaean), and Judas Iscariot, "...the one who betrayed Jesus" (Matthew 10:2-4). Writing as much as a decade or more after Mark's gospel,

Backfill

Luke lists the names in the following order along with a declaration of title: Simon (Peter), Andrew (his brother), James, John, Philip, Bartholomew, Matthew, Thomas, James (son of Alphaeus), Simon (called the Zealot), Judas (son of James), and Judas Iscariot "...who became the traitor" (Luke 6:14-16). At first glance, the contrasts among these three gospels appear minor. Still, on closer examination, the differences are anything but trivial and of marginal interest. First, only in Mark and Matthew does one find a reference to a tax collector being called to follow Jesus even before the actual naming of the twelve. However, Mark calls the man by the name of Levi, son of Alphaeus (Mark 2:14), while Matthew refers to the man as Matthew (Matthew 9:9). Mark's fellow writer, Matthew, fails to say that the tax collector listed in Mark's gospel is the same tax collector (Levi) in his gospel. Beyond this, Mark and Luke are the only two gospels to evidence the calling of disciples in "stages," including Simon (Peter), Andrew, James and John (Mark 1:16-20), and Simon (Peter), James and John (5:1-11), Levi (5:27), and the twelve (6:14-16). Besides, one finds no mention of Andrew as the brother of Simon (Peter) in Mark's gospel, and Luke has replaced Thaddaeus with Judas, son of James (Luke 6:16). As one explores the latest of the gospels, the gospel of John, there are yet other differences that appear. Early on, John refers to the group as "...the twelve..." (John 6:67). It is not until some fifteen chapters later when Jesus makes a post-resurrection appearance that John seems to fill-in-the-blanks by offering the names of several of his disciples, including Simon Peter, Thomas (the Twin), Nathanael (of Cana of Galilee), the sons of Zebedee, and two other disciples. Of interest here is the supposed addition of two disciples to the so-called list such as Thomas (the Twin) and Nathanael.

> *...the differences are anything but trivial and of marginal interest.*

Michael F. Price

Equally intriguing is John's mention of the remaining disciples also present for Jesus' Easter appearance. As John writes, also present were "...the sons of Zebedee, and two others of his disciples" (John 21:2). Once again, the later gospel writers take full advantage of the element of time to further "cloud" an already imprecise history.

One must also mention that the later gospel writers made use of the time between the appearance of Mark's gospel and the Johannine account to lessen the presence and influence of John the Baptist. Properly, John the Baptist's first appearance on the scene occurs early in the gospel of Mark as the Baptist is proclaimed as a messenger advocating baptism as a means of receiving forgiveness of sins. Clothed in camel hair and eating a diet of locusts and wild honey, he is baptizing individuals in the waters of the Jordan River. Mark is quick to point out the Baptist's position; namely, there is someone following John, who is more powerful than himself, and that person baptizes with the spirit while John does so with water. In time, not only does Jesus appear and is baptized by John, but the act is acknowledged by divine acclamation. The Baptist's presence in the opening scenes of Mark's gospel ends with John's arrest by Herod (1:1-11, 14). Following some questioning surrounding the question of why John's followers fast and the followers of Jesus do not (2:18-22), the next mention of John the Baptist in Mark's gospel occurs five chapters later as Mark records John's beheading at the hands of Herod. A lengthy discourse follows on John's arrest, imprisonment, and what happens to the Baptist's body upon his death (6:14-29). John is mentioned a fourth time in Mark's gospel around the time that Peter declares that Jesus is the Messiah (8:27-30). A fifth and final reference of John the Baptist in Mark's gospel is found not long after Jesus makes his triumphal entry into Jerusalem. Here, John's name is cited as chief priests, scribes, and elders question Jesus' authority (11:27-33). As one compares and contrasts the writings of the

Backfill

later three writers, it is apparent that with each gospel, there is a drop in the Baptists' position and prestige.

True to form, Matthew closely follows Mark's lead as it relates to the significant events in John's life, including

> ...*one can begin to see the laying of a foundation that seems to lessen John's role*...

the proclamation of the coming Messiah (3:17), the baptism of Jesus (3:13-17), the issue of fasting (9:14-17), the events surrounding the Baptist's arrest, imprisonment, and death at the hand of Herod (14:1-12), Peter's major declaration that Jesus is "...the Son of the Living God" (16:13-20), and the appearance of Jesus before the priests, scribes, and elders (21:23-27). There is one event involving John that's found in Matthew's gospel but not in Mark's and encompasses the exchange between John's followers and Jesus' divinity (Matthew 11:2-15). However, one can begin to see the laying of a foundation that seems to lessen John's role in the coming ministry of Jesus even though it's been a mere five decades or less since the passing of Jesus. For example, Matthew has the Baptist proclaiming there will be one coming along that is more powerful than he, and that John is not worthy even to carry this person's sandals (3:11).

As for Luke's gospel, it, too, has a parallel with Mark's gospel in several primary issues relating to John the Baptist. Just as we found in Mark's gospel, the proclamation of the coming Messiah (3:1-6), the baptism of Jesus (3:21-22), the exchange between John's followers and the followers of Jesus (7:18-23), and Peter's declaration (9:18-20), one finds those in Luke's gospel. Nevertheless, one quickly discovers that there are accounts in Luke's gospel that are absent from Mark's gospel, including the story of John the Baptist's birth (1:5-ff), the addendum following

> ...*the prayer we know today as the Lord's Prayer*...

John's proclamation in chapter 3 in which John calls those who had come out to be baptized vipers (3:7 – ff), and Herod's trepidation surrounding Jesus (9:7-9). As we have seen in Matthew's gospel, there is evidence in Luke's gospel that John the Baptist's role among the later gospel writers is becoming less-and-less significant. First, there is the effort by Jesus to add to the prayer that John was teaching his followers…the prayer we know today as the Lord's Prayer (11:2-4), and Peter's confession (9:18-20). The most damning of Luke's efforts to highlight John's shrinking role in the third gospel may well be the words of Jesus in which he seems to place John near the bottom of the pole of human importance (7:28b).

Most striking are the differences between Mark's view of the role of John the Baptist and the role that the last of the later gospel writers, John, has of the Baptist. Granted, there is the testimony of the Baptist (1:19-23), and the baptism of Jesus…implied but not detailed (1:29-34). But on closer review, John's perspective of the role and importance of John the Baptist comes early on. In the opening lines of his gospel, John is quick to point out that the Baptist came as a witness to testify to the light (1:7), that he (John the Baptist) was not the light (1:8), and the true light was coming (1:9). One finds further evidence in the same chapter as John writes that the Baptist proclaims that the one that comes after him ranks ahead of him (1:15). As further proof, the Baptist is asked three times by the priests and Levites if he is the Messiah, and three times John answers that he is not the Messiah (1:20-21). Two chapters later, John has the Baptist once again proclaiming that he is not the Messiah (3:28). A third time that John relegates the Baptist to a subordinate role to that of Jesus has Jesus saying that "…I (Jesus) have a testimony greater than John's" (5:36). Still, the proverbial nail-in-the-coffin that John the Baptist's role in the gospels was spiraling downward appears as John writes those famous words spoken by the Baptist that "He (Jesus) must increase, but I (John the Baptist) must decrease" (3:30). More, it is evident from the beginning of John's gospel until its end that the Baptist openly accepted his secondary role to Christ by repeatedly denying to be the light and that Jesus was more significant than he. It seems that what began in Matthew and continued in Luke has been thoroughly validated in John; namely, Jesus was on his way "up" while John the Baptist was on his way "down." While Matthew's gospel never explicitly conveys that John was the one that baptized Jesus, Luke also fails to mention who did the baptizing. By the time of John's gospel, the Baptist has been relegated as one who is bearing witness to the light. There is nothing of Jesus being baptized by John the Baptist in John's gospel.

Summary: It is apparent that the later gospel writers sought to bring a degree of harmony to that of Mark's writings. The inclusion of communal stories includes but is not limited to the proclamation of John the Baptist, the baptism of Jesus, the calling of the first disciples, the feeding of the 5,000, the arrest, imprisonment, and death of John the Baptist, Peter's declaration, Judas's betrayal of Jesus, Jesus' triumphal entry into Jerusalem, and the most epic of these stories, Jesus' resurrection. Less obvious but equally as intentional are the efforts of Matthew, Luke, and John to exploit the element of time to backfill their endeavors at transforming Jesus into the Risen Christ. From the opening chapters in Matthew's gospel which closely correspond to the unfolding events in Mark's gospel in which the Baptist proclaims that there will be one coming along that is more powerful than he, to the comparable passages from Luke's gospel that seems to place John near the bottom of the pole of human importance, and finally to the

> *...the later gospel writers took it upon themselves to change, yea invent, the narrative and backfill as they went...*

words of John that state that Jesus' role must increase at the same time the Baptist's must decrease, the proof that the later gospel writers took full advantage of the half-century between the appearance of Mark's gospel and John's gospel is beyond reproach. Jesus did not seem to fit the likely model of a Savior and a Messiah, so the later gospel writers took it upon themselves to change, yea invent, the narrative and backfill as they went, beginning with Matthew's gospel and culminating in John's gospel. More, the later gospel writers were not only intentional but highly successful in their efforts to take the fundamental facts of Mark's gospel, massage these facts, adding or deleting as they saw fit, to continue their efforts in transforming the historical Jesus into someone of a higher divinity. And it seems the further-and-further each of the later gospel writers was away from the actual events surrounding Jesus' life, the more they embellished. What began in Mark's gospel as Jesus being "adopted" by God has since moved to Jesus being "born" divine in Matthew and Luke to Jesus being the Logos of God in John's gospel…and all of this unfolds in less than seventy-five years! Without a doubt, the later gospel writers used the gaps in time from the death of Jesus to the time each of these writers produced their work to their advantage. The more that time moved on, the less the facts surrounding Jesus' life could be verified by others. Without any people or means to check what was true or not, the more Matthew, Luke, and John were free to embroider Mark's gospel.

However, the element of time was not the only element of time that the later gospel writer utilized to further their Christology. Equally impressive was the gospel writer's utilization of *context*.

Chapter Four

Context

*"Reality is not a function of the event as event,
but of the relationship of that event to past,
and future, events."
(Robert Penn Warren)*

As we prepare to explore the second of the three elements that the later gospel writers utilized to backfill their particular gospel, I'm thinking of the story of the country minister that visits a church member one Sunday afternoon. Moments after arriving, the preacher is asked by the family matriarch if they would read aloud a few passages from the scriptures. Just then, the matriarch asks one of her grandsons to please "go and bring the good book from the table so the reverend can read to us." Confused as to which book he was supposed to bring back, the child seeks some clarity. "Which book is that?" the child asks. "You know," the grandmother answers, "the big book that we love and read from all the time." With that, the grandson heads out of the family living room. Moments later, the child returns with a copy of the Sears and Roebuck catalog.

I know, old and trite, but this story does make a point; namely, the context in which something takes place has a significant influence on our understanding of things. And as we shall quickly learn, the later gospel writers we know as Matthew, Luke, and John, take full advantage of the context in which they were writing to shape, mold, and advance their efforts to transform the historical Jesus to the Risen Christ. Of the many examples in the gospels that further this understanding, the one that quickly comes to mind involves

Michael F. Price

the last words of Jesus from the cross.

Set in the context of that day Christians know as Good Friday, the oldest of the gospels, the Gospel of Mark, records that Jesus has not only appeared before Pilate in the early morning hours, but he (Pilate) allows Jesus' fate to be decided by an unruly crowd that has chosen a criminal by the name of Barabbas to be freed ahead of Jesus. Consequently, Jesus is sentenced to be crucified. At 9:00am, at the place called Golgotha, Jesus is placed between two bandits, one to the left of him and one to his right. At noon, Mark writes that darkness came across the whole land until 3:00pm. Then, at 3:00pm, Jesus cries out in a loud voice, "Eloi, Eloi, lema sabachthani?" According to Mark, these are the lone words Jesus speaks from the cross (15:34).

In his gospel, Matthew records the events surrounding the death of Jesus differently. Following an appearance before Caiaphas, the high priest, Jesus appears before Pilate at some point on the morning of Good Friday. Using the backdrop of Mark's story, Matthew has Pilate ask the crowd whom he (Pilate) should release, Jesus or Barabbas. The crowd replies that Pilate should release Barabbas and crucify Jesus. After arriving at Golgotha, Jesus is placed on a cross that is placed between the crosses of two bandits, one on his left and one on his right, who proceed to taunt Jesus. From 12:00 noon until 3:00 pm, darkness covers the land. At 3:00 pm, and following nearly to a "T" the words of Mark, Matthew writes that Jesus cries out in a loud voice, "Eli, Eli, lama sabachthani." Similar to Mark, these are the only words that Matthew records that Jesus says from the cross (27:46).

> *...these are the only words that Matthew records that Jesus says from the cross...*

Attempting to put his slant on the epic events of that day, Luke writes that things went down in this fashion. First, Jesus is brought before a council comprised of chief priests and

Backfill

scribes, then to Pilate, and finally Herod. Backfilling with some of the same elements from Mark, such as the question of whom to release, Jesus or Barabbas, the crowd votes to release Barabbas and crucify Jesus. Almost immediately, Pilate commands that Jesus be taken to the place called the Skull. Upon arriving, Jesus is placed on the cross, and the cross is stationed between the crosses containing two criminals. Luke then shares that Jesus speaks the first of three sentences, including "Father, forgive them; for they do not know what they are doing" (23:34). Sometime later, Jesus speaks a second time from the cross. Replying to a request from one of the criminals surrounding him seeking inclusion into the coming kingdom, Jesus replies, saying: "Truly I tell you, today you will be with me in Paradise" (23:43). Still later in the afternoon, Jesus speaks his third, and final, words from the cross: "Father, into your hands I commend my spirit" (23:46).

Finally, John has the events of that first Good Friday unfolding this way. Following somewhat the lead of Mark, Jesus appears first before Caiaphas, then Pilate, and finally to the crowd, which votes to free Barabbas and crucify Jesus. After being led to Golgotha, Jesus is placed on a cross with two others, each to the side of him on their crosses. In time, Jesus speaks three sentences, including "Woman, here is your son...here is your mother," "I am thirsty," and "It is finished" (18:26-19:30).

Generally speaking, there are several common elements among the four gospels relating to the passion narrative, including, Jesus appearing before the Sanhedrin, Jesus delivered to Pilate, the trial before Pilate, the question of Jesus or Barabbas, Pilate delivers Jesus to be crucified, the road to Golgotha, the placement of Jesus' cross between the crosses of two others who were also being crucified, the mocking of Jesus by the soldiers, the crucifixion, and the death of Jesus. Conversely, there are other passages among the narrative that appear in specific gospels, including, Jesus ridiculed by

Michael F. Price

onlookers (Matthew 27:38-43, Mark 15:27-32, Luke 23:35-38), and the taunting by one, or both, of the thieves (Matthew 27:44, Luke 23:39-43). The gospel of Luke remains the only gospel to mention Jesus appearing before Herod and Pilate's declaration that Jesus is innocent (23:6-12, 13-16).

Far and above, the most intriguing aspect of the passion narrative is the way each of the gospel writers utilizes Jesus' crucifixion on Golgotha, and particularly his last seven sentences, to backfill the details of their specific gospel further.

The widely accepted belief is that Jesus spoke seven sentences from the cross during the six hours he hung there before being taken down. However, the seven sentences are spread out among the four gospels such that no one gospel contains all seven sentences. Of the seven sentences, three appear in John's gospel, and three in Luke's gospel. In contrast, the fourth of Jesus' last sentences from the cross is located in both the gospel of Matthew and Mark's gospel. The traditional order of the seven sentences include…

> *…no one gospel contains all seven sentences.*

"Truly I tell you, today you will be with me in Paradise" (Luke 23:34)

"Father, forgive them; for they do not know what they are doing" (Luke 23:43)

"Woman, here is your son . . . Here is your mother" (John 19:26-27)

"My God, my God, why have you forsaken me?" (Mark 15:34, Matthew 27:46)

"I am thirsty" (John 19:28)

"It is finished" (John 19:30)

"Father, into your hands I commend my spirit" (Luke 23:46)

The first thing that one notices is that the arrangement of

Backfill

these seven sentences seems to *begin in the perimeter* (Luke 23:34, Luke 23:46), continues inward toward the most historical of the sentences (Mark 15:34), *packing and layering* along the way (Matthew 23:43), and adding *small pieces of refill to create a better quality backfill* (John 19:26-30). Granted, the gospel writers had no say in the sequence of the sentences. Still, the order is uncanny, especially as one considers that the later gospel writers (Matthew and Luke) "borrowed" much of the content of their gospels from Mark. At the same time, John may have had a working knowledge of Mark's words. Remember, John's gospel may have been written as much as three decades after Mark's was written!

And speaking of Mark's gospel, it's worth noting that Matthew seems to "spin" Jesus' words from the cross, as found in Mark's gospel, to fit Matthew's developing Christology. The centerpiece of the last seven words of Jesus' from the cross is commonly translated as "My God, my god, why have you forsaken me?" (Mark 15:34, Matthew 27:46). Mark records those words as "Eloi, Eloi, lema sabachthani." At the same time, Matthew says that Jesus' words were more along the line of "Eli, Eli, lema sabachthani" and that Jesus was calling for the prophet, Elijah. Additionally, Matthew's Jewish audience would recognize these words as being from Psalm 22, which begins, appropriately enough, "My God, my God, why have you forsaken me?" It could just be that Matthew manipulated Jesus' words to sound as if Jesus was calling to Elijah...Eli, for short...to lend credence to Matthew's premise that Jesus is the long-awaited Jewish messiah. Contemporary writers may term Matthew's tactic as "playing to his (Jewish) base." A further example of the later gospel writers playing to his audience includes John translating "rabboni" (Aramaic) in Greek (1:38), "Messiah" into "Anointed/Christ" (1:41), and "Cephas" into "Peter" (1:42).

> *...Matthew seems to "spin" Jesus' words from the cross...*

Michael F. Price

A third example of the way that the later gospel writers used the element of context to backfill their efforts to transform the historical Jesus into the Risen Christ is more simplistic and less thought-provoking. With pinpoint precision, the later gospel writers utilized the brevity of Mark's gospel as the perfect opportunity to *allow the curing of Mark's gospel to begin.* Following, Matthew, Luke, and John, then started to *blend in their words* with the words of Mark by inserting some of their sayings and stories about Jesus. As shared earlier, Mark's gospel contains 15 chapters and approximately 678 verses, making it the shortest of the four gospels. The gospels of Matthew and Luke contain 28 chapters and 1,071 verses and 24 chapters and 1,151 verses, respectively. In other words, Matthew's work is nearly twice as extensive in regards to chapters than Mark's gospel, with over 50% more verses. By comparison, Luke's gospel has 60% more chapters than Mark's gospel and nearly 75% more verses. The same stands true for the last of the four gospels, since there are roughly one-third more chapters in John's gospel (21) than in Mark's writings, and about the same as it relates to verses. If one compares the number of words in Mark's gospel to those used by the later writers, the numbers are equally revealing. John uses nearly 40% more words than Mark does in his gospel, Matthew over 60% more words, while Luke uses a whopping 70% more words in his gospel than that which one finds in Mark's gospel. Among the new additions one finds in Matthew's gospel beyond that which one finds in Mark's gospel, include the forty-two generations of ancestors (1:2-17), and the 107 verses and 2,000 words of the Sermon on the Mount (5:1-7:29). As for Luke's additions, the list contains the fifteen lines of Jesus' genealogy (3:23-38), and the parables of the Good Samaritan (10:25-37), the Prodigal Son

> *John uses nearly 40% more words than Mark does...*

Backfill

(15:11-32), and the cleansing of the ten lepers (17:11-19). The figurative "filler" in John's gospel comprises the pre-existence of Christ as the Logos (1:1-18), the story of the Samaritan woman Jesus meets at the well (4:4-26), and the story involving Jesus and the woman caught in adultery (8:2-11).

One should also mention the contextual efforts of the later gospel writers to take full advantage of a particular situation and work to move past the reference of Jesus as a criminal and toward that of seeing him as Christ. As the oldest of the gospel writers record it, "And with him they crucified two bandits, one on his right and one on his left" (Mark 15:26), and "Those who were crucified with him also taunted him" (15:32b). Matthew's version reads, "Then two bandits were crucified with him, one on his right and one on his left" (27:38), and "The bandits who were crucified with him also taunted him the same way" (27:44). Luke's understanding of Jesus' encounter with the two thieves, however, seems to convey the empathetic and compassionate side of Jesus coming to the surface. With the soldiers that were near him, Jesus speaks as one indeed sent from God and displaying uniquely divine characteristics, saying, "...Father, forgive them; for they do not know what they are doing" (23:34). Then, as one of the thieves begins deriding Jesus, demanding to see a sign that Jesus is the messiah, the second thief rebukes the first thief. Then he (the second thief) pleads with Jesus to remember him in the coming kingdom. Jesus' response: "Truly, I tell you, today you will be with me in Paradise" (23:32-43). Attempting to further his labors at elevating Jesus to a place of divinity, John writes in his gospel that Jesus was taken to Golgotha where they "...crucified him, and with him two others, one on either side" ((19:18). Did you catch that? While Mark, Matthew, and Luke state that Jesus was crucified between two bandits/thieves, John refrains from saying that the two individuals surrounding Jesus were even crooks! A subtle, yet powerful, utilization by John to use the element of context to backfill his gospel further and to prove his point that Jesus was the Christ. Otherwise, Jesus is just another criminal crucified alongside two other criminals. Jesus is guilty by association.

As further evidence of the later gospel writers' utilization of context to further their efforts of transforming Jesus from preacher to all-powerful, one must mention the dramatic events that happened not long after Jesus has spent his last breath. When the sixth hour of Jesus' presence upon the cross had arrived, darkness covered the whole land for three hours. At the ninth hour, Mark states that Jesus lets out a loud cry and draws his last breath. Suddenly, the curtain in the temple, the symbol of the chasm between creation's wickedness and God's holiness, was torn in two, from top to bottom. Then, a centurion, standing nearby, spoke, saying, "Truly this man was God's Son!" (Mark 15:33-39).

Using Mark's description as a starting point, Matthew seeks to add more description to the monumental event by adding some *small pieces of refill* to seemingly "spice up" his belief of Jesus' divinity. For three hours following the sixth hour, Matthew records that darkness covers the land. Next, Jesus cries out in a loud voice and then yields up his spirit. At nearly the same time, the temple curtain tears in two, the earth shakes, rocks are split, tombs open, and the saints that have passed on begin appearing in the holy city. Commenting on what had just happened, a centurion, and others who were with him that had seen what had taken place, declare that "Truly this was the Son of God!" (Matthew 27:45-54). In dramatic fashion, and for clarity, Matthew adds the following backfill. First, Matthew says that in addition to the tearing of the curtain, there is a shaking of the earth, splitting of rocks, opening of tombs, resurrection of souls, and a mass showing of these resurrected souls in the holy city. To lend further credence to his edition of this epic event, Matthew adds that the centurion was not the only one that

> *"Truly this was the Son of God."*

saw all this happening, because there were "…those who were with him…" (27:54).

In a somewhat abbreviated version of the immediate events following the death of Jesus on the cross, Luke agrees that there was darkness covering the land from the sixth to the ninth hour. While he fails to seemingly follow the lead of his fellow writer Matthew by mentioning a shaking earth, splitting rocks, and revived souls, Luke, nevertheless, uses the context to further promote his understanding of Jesus' divinity by adding not only the centurion's belief that Jesus was innocent but that multitudes observed what had happened on that first Good Friday (23:47).

Not to be outdone in his understanding of the events of that day, John seeks to *blend in* his backfill but not in a way one might expect. Consequently, John includes nothing that we might expect from the gospels of the three other writers. Instead, John jumps from Jesus saying his last words to the soldiers that were standing nearby to the soldiers piercing the sides of Jesus' body to make sure he was dead. As blood and water ooze from Jesus' lifeless body, John writes parenthetically that "He who saw this has testified so that you may also believe. His testimony is true, and he knows that he tells the truth" (John 19:34-35).

> *…no mention of the town of Bethlehem and only limited citations…*

Last but not least, it's worth mentioning the later gospel writers' efforts to backfill the events between both Jesus' birth and his death. Specifically, the reference to the towns of Bethlehem and Nazareth. Accordingly, there is no mention of the town of Bethlehem and only limited citations to "Jesus of Nazareth" in Mark's entire gospel. Of the handful of mentionings (5), the first revolves around his baptism (1:9). The second comes from a man with an unclean spirit asking why Jesus is in the synagogue in Capernaum (1:24). The remaining references center on the healing of the blind

Michael F. Price

Bartimaeus in Jericho (10:47), Peter's denial of Jesus (14:67), and the declaration of the young man, dressed in white, on that first Easter morning: "…Do not be alarmed, you are looking for Jesus of Nazareth, who was crucified. He has been raised; he is not here…" (16:5). Conversely, Matthew, seeking to not only make full use of the decades following the writing of Mark's gospel by utilizing the element of context to his advantage while also playing to his Jewish base, alludes to the historic city of Bethlehem, the city of King David, a total of four times. All appear in the second chapter of his gospel surrounding the birth of Jesus (2:1, 2:5-6, 2:16).

Meanwhile, Matthew cites the city of Nazareth four times in his gospel. The first reference is found in the second chapter (2:23), and the second as Jesus leaves his home in Nazareth to begin his ministry (4:13). In contrast, the remaining two references occur in the last quarter of his gospel (21:11, 26:71). Luke appears to initially "take the bait" that Matthew offers regarding the birth of Jesus in Bethlehem, but does him one better by adding his own backfill to Matthew's backfill! After mentioning that Jesus' birth takes place in the city of Bethlehem (2:4), the city's name does not appear again in Luke's gospel.

Henceforth, Luke seems to cut-his-own-path by seemingly working to elevate Jesus' connection to Nazareth over that of Bethlehem. First by mentioning the town of Nazareth in the foretelling of Jesus' birth by the angel Gabriel (1:26) and then by frontloading Matthew's words regarding the decree from Emperor Augustus for males to return to their hometown to register, Luke seeks to get the jump on Matthew's version of the birth narrative by promoting Nazareth over Bethlehem by adding that "Joseph also went from the town of Nazareth in Galilee, to Judea, to the city of David called Bethlehem…" (2:3-4). Equally convincing are Luke's efforts to

> *…by frontloading Matthew's words…*

Backfill

further elevate the importance of Nazareth over Bethlehem in the remainder of his gospel, including the presentation of Jesus in the temple (2:39), his teaching in the temple and the family's subsequent trip to Nazareth (2:51), Jesus' rejection "...in the town where he had been brought up..." (4:16), the questioning of the man with an unclean spirit (4:34), the plea of the blind man for sight (18:37), and the appearance of Jesus to the two men along the Emmaus Road (24:19).

True to form, John, seeking to limit Jesus' birth connection to anything earthly, does not mention the town of Bethlehem even once in his gospel. In contrast, the town of Nazareth is cited four times...the first surrounding the calling of Philip and Nathanael (1:45), the rhetorical and derogatory question from Nathanael to Philip "...Can anything good come out of Nazareth?" (1:46), the betrayal of Judas and arrest of Jesus (18:5-7), and the words that Pilate had inscribed and put on the cross of Jesus that read "Jesus of Nazareth, the King of the Jews" (19:19).

Summary: Mark did not invent the historical Jesus any more than he did Mary, the mother of Jesus, John the Baptist, or any other character found among the pages of the four gospels. Mark simply revealed Jesus' life, ministry, death, and resurrection to the world. Not content with Mark's understanding of Jesus, the later gospel writers took it upon themselves to do one better. Subsequently, Matthew, Luke, and John take the historical Jesus in Mark's gospel, utilize the element of context, and make Jesus of equal divinity with God. Backfilling when possible to fit their evolving Christology, the later gospel writers begin their efforts with Jesus' resurrection and work backward, utilizing all situations to their benefit.

Mark mentions nothing in his gospel about the baby Jesus or Bethlehem, nothing about travel and evil trappings by wicked rulers, and nothing about ancestors and biological associates of Jesus. The closest reference to Jesus' birthplace

Michael F. Price

in Mark's gospel mentions Nazareth and not Bethlehem (1:9).

But Matthew, taking full advantage of his context and the lack of anyone to dispute his understanding of events, seems to tack-on not only to the back of Mark's Jesus story by offering a different account of Jesus' resurrection but also to the front of the story. Of the later gospel writers, it is Matthew who first employs the element of context to tell his story of Jesus. Matthew begins by recording that Jesus is born to a virgin (1:23) in the historic city of Bethlehem (2:5-6). Next, he includes a visit of the wise men (2:1-12), followed by the family of Jesus escaping to Egypt (2:13-15) to avoid infanticide at the hands of Herod (2:16-18). Matthew seeks to convince his Jewish audience that Jesus is more than an itinerate preacher. In Jesus, one not only finds the second coming of Moses but the long-awaited messiah sent from God to create a level playing field in the lives of the Jewish community.

In an effort that seems to do Matthew one better, Luke takes Matthew's version of things and frontloads Matthew's story with the foretelling of the birth of John the Baptist (1:5-25), the visit of Mary to her relative, Elizabeth (1:39-45), the birth of John the Baptist, the one who will eventually baptize Jesus (1:57-66), and the proclamation to the shepherds "…who were keeping watch over their flock by night" (2:8-20). Likewise, one quickly notices from the gospel of Luke an attempt to mitigate Mary's position as an unwed female by introducing the concept that Mary was impregnated by the Holy Spirit (1:26-38).

> *Matthew seeks to convince his Jewish audience that Jesus is more than an itinerate preacher.*

Once the gospels of Matthew and Luke are complete, there is no further mention of Bethlehem in the gospels. Moreover, one will discover that in John's gospel, there is no mention of a virgin birth, the holy city of Bethlehem, wise men, shepherds, or an emergency trip to Egypt by Jesus and his

Backfill

family. Instead, John seems to backfill by sharing that Jesus was with God from the beginning.

Conversely, one seems to find the opposite thing happening as it relates to the town of Nazareth. As the later gospel writers endeavor to transform the historical Jesus into the Risen Christ, Nazareth appears to increase in importance as Bethlehem's significance seemingly decreases. The name "Nazareth" is mentioned twenty times in the gospels, including five times in Mark's gospel, four times in Matthew's understanding of Jesus' life, four times in John's writings, and an impressive seven times in Luke's words. The reasons for utilizing the small, sleepy town to their advantage are apparent.

First, it turns out that Nazareth was the perfect context to highlight as having historical significance in Jesus' life. Prior to the second century, Nazareth was nothing more than a small village, so there was no way that others could argue Jesus' history in, or with, the town. There were no records to fact-check about Jesus' birth, and less likely that those that may have known him were still alive some 50 – 75 years after his birth. What better way to direct a narrative and transform a person like Jesus into the most significant figure in Christian history than to introduce the belief that he was from a small and quiet town in Galilee that had limited, if any, birth records. Subsequently, two of the three later gospel writers (Luke and John) took full advantage of Jesus' association with the town of Nazareth.

> *What better way to direct a narrative and transform a person like Jesus into the most significant figure in Christian history...*

In like manner, all three of the later gospel writers (Matthew, Luke, and John) seem to take full advantage of the fact that there were few, if any, who could test these writers' understanding of events in the life of Jesus or even their approach to sharing the story. The advent of the records of

Michael F. Price

Matthew, Luke, and John appear at a time when it was all but impossible to check the authenticity of the facts, the sequence of events, who was involved, or what was said. As the gatekeepers of this information, the later gospel writers may have perceived that spreading the word of the life, ministry, and resurrection of Jesus was more important to these writers than getting the facts right. And if the events were at a minimum, these three writers had no problem with backfilling, however preliminary or conflicting their version maybe with the narrative of the other gospel writers. Furthermore, those that may have chosen to contest the words of these later writers to determine the accuracy of what was being shared had no written documents upon which to base their allegations. If others understood the facts of Matthew, Luke, and John to be wrong, it would take a monumental effort of time and energy to correct them. By the time any inaccuracies, contradictions, or discrepancies in the texts were noticed, it was too late…the gospels had become "canonized"… at least in the minds of those that were living in the first and second centuries. Once the teachings and events in the life of Jesus become written, there was little chance of challenging or arguing theology, reviewing the facts, hearing from those that disagreed, the presence of any kind of avenue of discussion, or stopping the gospel's dissemination. The horse was out of the barn, so good luck corralling it!

By the same token, it appears that the later gospel writers took full advantage of the general absence of anything written, including books, to propagate their Christology. The scarcity of books, along with the fact that books were copied one-by-one, which meant the process of reproduction was time-consuming and drawn-out, also played to the advantage of these three writers. Subsequently, to get

> *…the process of reproduction was time-consuming and drawn-out, also played to the advantage of these three writers.*

Backfill

one's work out front and circulating as soon as possible was vital for these writers and their particular efforts. If your written work was published first, there was a good chance it would become the standard in content, since the dissemination and the trickle-down effect of the written word to the smaller and less populated areas like Nazareth was commonly slower. And if that work was made relevant to the general population, say, farmers, artisans, carpenters, fishermen, and the so-called working class, used contemporary language rather than obscure words and phrases, parables that most people could connect to, and fit situations that were familiar like fields, vineyards, and fishing, the chances of that work being generally accepted was significantly increased. Add to this the high probability of illiteracy, and it seems that the later gospel writers could not have found themselves in a more favorable position and a more promising context in which to advance their theology. This is to say nothing of the fact that people lived outside…way outside…of the places where these stories of miracles of people being raised from the dead, fish being multiplied, and ministry to the men and women on the margins of society, had happened. It was the ideal crowd, content, and context, and it seems that the later gospel writers took full advantage of all three of these elements.

In all, it seems that Matthew, Luke, and John could do their thing without thought of consequences, retribution, or impunity. The lack of any corroborative evidence beyond that of Mark's gospel to compare texts not only opened the door for these three later writers but offered them a free pass to embellish, manipulate, and alter events and people into a mosaic of their liking. Moreover, these writers may have seen themselves free of all social, political, or religious constraints. Matthew, Luke, and John had a blank page and utilized this context to their benefit. They could write without restriction, reserve, resistance, or resignation. Swimmers call such a place "smooth waters."

Michael F. Price

Chapter Five

Cause

*"Work for a cause
and not applause."*
(Anonymous)

As we arrive at the third and final factor that the later gospel writers capitalized upon to backfill their respective gospels, it has hopefully become apparent that these writers were not seeking fame or fortune. Their initial efforts were to simply get the word out regarding the life, ministry, death, and resurrection of Jesus. Little did they know, or expect, that their work would shape and mold a religious movement that would reach to nearly every corner of the world. But as the years increased following the death of Jesus, there may have been a mounting interest for a deeper understanding of his life and teachings, elements seemingly absent in Mark's gospel. Consequently, the later gospel writers seemed to stumble upon a third element that they would utilize to further their efforts to transform the historical Jesus into the Risen Christ. The element of *cause*.

> **The element of cause.**

Historically speaking, Matthew seems to be the first of the later gospel writers to note this growing interest to learn more about the itinerate preacher from Nazareth. In response, it appears that Matthew was more than willing to supply answers for the increasing demand to know more about Jesus. However, those answers may have been highly biased, less-than-fact filled, and overtly subjective. Just as it was for his fellow gospel writers, Matthew firstly transferred much of

Backfill

what Mark had written about Jesus to his narrative. Following, Matthew then backfills into his gospel with his own understanding of people, places, and proclamations.

Matthew ostensibly begins his efforts at backfilling Mark's gospel by *going to the perimeter and working inward*. For example, Matthew modifies Mark's narrative of the events surrounding that first Easter morning. Mark records that the time of day as being "…very early on the first day of the week, when the sun had risen…" (16:2), that it was "…Mary Magdalene, and Mary the mother of James, and Salome…" that make the trek to the tomb where Jesus had been laid (16:1), and their reason for making their way to the tomb of Jesus "…so that they may go and anoint him" (16:1-2). Asking themselves who will roll away the stone placed at the entrance to the tomb, the women discover upon arriving that the stone has already been moved to the side. As they enter, they see a young man dressed in a white robe, sitting inside. The young man tells the women not to be afraid; Jesus has been raised and is no longer there. Mark concludes his understanding of the events surrounding Jesus' resurrection by saying that the young man then tells the women to not only go and tell the disciples and Peter that Jesus is going ahead of them to Galilee but also that he (Jesus) will meet them there. In response, the women take off from the tomb but end up saying nothing to anyone "…for they were afraid" (16:3-8). The more extended ending of Mark has Jesus appearing to Mary along with her returning to tell the others that she had seen the Risen Christ. "But when they heard that he was alive and had been seen by her, they would not believe it" (16:9-10). However, Matthew records the event differently in his gospel.

Matthew writes that it was "…as the first day of the week was dawning, Mary Magdalene and the other Mary went to see the tomb" (28:1). Suddenly, there is a great earthquake; "…for an angel of the Lord, descending from heaven, came and rolled back the stone and sat on it" (28:2). The appearance of this angel was like lightning, and the clothing was such a dazzling white that it caused the guards to shake like dead men. The angel then speaks to the women telling them not to be afraid because the crucified Jesus has been raised, but also for the women to come and see where Jesus was laid prior.

> *Whereas Mark begins his narrative of the life of Jesus with Jesus' baptism...*

Matthew then records that the angel tells the women to go and say to his disciples that he (Jesus) will meet them in Galilee. As the women leave the tomb with joy and excitement, they are met by Jesus. The women promptly take hold of Jesus' feet and begin worshipping him. Matthew closes his version of Jesus' resurrection with Jesus once again telling the women not to be afraid, but to also share the message for "...my brothers to go to Galilee; there they will see me (Jesus)" (28:3-10).

In like manner, Matthew also frontloads Mark's gospel. Whereas Mark begins his narrative of the life of Jesus with Jesus' baptism, Matthew lists the genealogy of Jesus followed by the dream of Joseph and Jesus' soon to be birth (1:1-ff). Matthew suddenly shifts to the visit of the wise men to Herod, the family's escape to Egypt so Jesus could avoid Herod's slaughter and the subsequent return of the family of Jesus to Nazareth (2:1-ff). From there, Matthew *utilizes much of the existing material* of Mark's gospel, beginning with John the Baptist's proclamation for repentance.

In between the bookends of Matthew's story, the writer seeks to backfill with additional episodes to support his developing Christology. Absent from Mark's writings but evident in Matthew's narrative are small pieces of *new and layered aggregate, packed,* as *further support*, including the story of the

> *...small pieces of new and layered aggregate, packed, as further support,...*

Backfill

two blind men who seek healing from Jesus (9:27-31), the account of the mother of James and John as she pleads for her sons to have a special place in Jesus' coming kingdom (20:20-28), and the parable of the two sons who have opposing views of working in the vineyard (21:28-32). Throughout his gospel, it seems clear that Matthew is successful in *blending in* additional examples of Jesus' mercy and compassion, the requirements of discipleship, and forgiveness, all to meet the growing demands to know more about the spiritual side of this man from Galilee.

Several years later, it looks as if it's Luke's turn to seemingly backfill Matthew's gospel as Luke endeavors to address questions that have surfaced regarding Jesus' life. Luke begins on the *perimeter and works inward*. At one edge of his gospel, Luke takes it upon himself to rewrite the events of Jesus' resurrection. First, Luke writes that it's "...the first day of the week, at early dawn..." and "...they came to the tomb taking the spices they had prepared" (24:1). We are not told until nine verses later that the "they" in the story are "...Mary Magdalene, Joanna, Mary the mother of James, and the other women with them..." (24:10). Upon arriving, the women find the stone at the entrance to the tomb rolled away, so they go inside. However, Jesus' body is gone. Confused, the women suddenly find themselves in the presence of two men who are dressed in clothes and standing beside them. As the women fall to the ground, they are asked why they are looking for the living Jesus because he (Jesus) has risen. The women are reminded that they were told that Jesus would be handed over to sinners, be crucified, and on the third day be raised. Leaving the tomb, the women return to the eleven and the rest. Luke closes his description of that first Easter morning by writing that when the women tell the others what had happened, the women's words are not believed. One of the disciples, Peter, suddenly gets up and begins making his way toward the empty tomb. Elated that the only thing that he sees is the linen wrappings that used to cover Jesus, Peter departs, "...amazed at what had happened" (24:2-12).

At the opposite end of his gospel, Luke makes clear early on that he has "...decided, after investigating everything carefully from the very first, to write an orderly account..." (1:3). Frontloading Matthew's gospel, Luke begins with the forecast of the birth of John the Baptist to a priest

> *...utilizes much of the existing material...but includes small pieces to create better backfill.*

named Zechariah and his wife, Elizabeth, followed by the visit of an angel to an unmarried, pregnant woman living in Nazareth, named Mary, telling her that she is carrying the Son of God, and finally, the announcement of the birth of John the Baptist. As Luke's unique addition continues, he highlights the journey of Joseph and Mary to Bethlehem, the declaration of the birth of Jesus to the shepherds, the naming and presentation of Jesus in the temple, the returning of Jesus' family to Nazareth, and the discovery of Jesus in the temple as he teaches those in attendance. From there, Luke not only *utilizes much of the existing material* from Mark's gospel just as Matthew did decades earlier in his gospel but includes *small pieces to create better backfill*. To deepen the understandings of the unique traits of Jesus that Mark and Matthew may have overlooked, Luke seeks to *blend in* several exclusive stories of Jesus' ability to instill confidence and trust in him (5:4-7), his deep compassion to care for the oppressed, the poor and those on the margins of society (10:30-37), along with his divine ability to heal the blind and the ailing (13:10-17).

Nearly a century after the birth of Jesus and a full half-century following the writing of Mark's gospel, the opportunity presents itself for the last of the gospel writers to have his say in addressing the increasing questions regarding the life of Jesus. As expected, the last of the gospel writers takes his lead from Matthew and Luke as he begins his efforts

Backfill

at transforming the historical Jesus into the Risen Christ on the *perimeter and works inward.*

John begins on the southside of his gospel with a reconstruction of Jesus' resurrection. *Utilizing some of the existing material* from Mark, John writes, it's "Early on the first day of the week, while it was still dark, Mary Magdalene came to the tomb and saw that the stone had been removed from the tomb" (20:1). As John begins to *include small pieces of aggregate to create a better backfill,* he states that Mary Magdalene rushes to tell Simon Peter and another of the disciples that the body of Jesus is gone. Mary is unsure where Jesus' body has been placed. Immediately, Peter and the other disciple, the one that Jesus loved, set out for the empty tomb. The other disciple arrives first, but after looking into the tomb, he decides to wait for Peter before doing anything. When Peter arrives, he enters the tomb and finds only the remnants of the wrappings that once covered Jesus' body. Shortly after that, the other disciple enters the tomb and discovers the same. John then closes the first of two Easter morning paragraphs writing, "Then the disciples returned to their home" (20:2-10).

Seeking further to *pack the material* in his narrative, John follows up his first words by recording that not only has Mary Magdalene arrived on the scene, but she, too, looks inside the now-empty tomb. There, she sees two angels sitting where the body of Jesus once laid. When asked by the angels why she is crying, Mary responds by saying that "...they have taken away my Lord, and I do not know where they have laid him" (20:11-13). Turning around, she sees Jesus standing there, but Mary fails to recognize him. Jesus asks Mary the same question that was asked by the angels. Believing the figure to be the gardener, Mary then pleads with the gardener where she might find the body of Jesus. After Jesus calls her name, Mary recognizes that it's the Risen Christ! Asking Mary to not hold onto him as he (Jesus) has yet to ascend to the Father, John includes one final effort in his understanding of the events;

namely, Jesus instructions for Mary to return to the disciples so that she can announce the good news of her encounter with the Risen Christ (20:14-18).

Following the route of his counterparts, John makes a change to the first pages of his gospel...and it's nothing less than monumental. John writes that "In the beginning was the Word, and the Word was with God, and the Word was God. He was in the beginning with God...He came to what was his own, and his own people did not accept him. But to all who received him, who believed in his name, he gave power to become children of God...And the Word became flesh and lived among us, and we have seen his glory, the glory as of a father's only son, full of grace and truth" (1:1-14). Sandwiched between the first appearance of the Logos onto the scene and the resurrection of Jesus, John seeks to *blend in* stories that demonstrate the ultimate divinity of Jesus. Included in his efforts to *pack the material* to create a better backfill while at the same time elevating Christ's uniqueness, John highlights explicitly the miracle of Jesus changing of the water into wine at the wedding in Cana (2:1-11), Jesus' encounter with the woman at the well (4:4-26), and Jesus' supreme act of forgiveness for the woman caught in adultery (7:53-8:11).

> *...John makes a change to the first pages of his gospel...and it's nothing less than monumental.*

A second cause utilized by the later gospel writers to promote their narrative of transforming the historical Jesus into the Risen Christ centers on the efforts of these writers to reinforce Mark's information regarding Jesus' divinity, and if need be, redact it.

In the vast majority of the Markan texts, Jesus seeks to diminish any references to himself as either the Messiah or the Son of God. Time after time, one finds among the pages of Mark's gospel several instances where Jesus seems to avoid;

Backfill

yea downright rejects any reference to himself as the Messiah. When a healing miracle does take place, Mark's Jesus immediately pleads with those around him not to tell anyone what had taken place. The instances of Jesus' stern plea follow the healing of a man of leprosy (1:40-44), the healing of Jairus' daughter (5:21-24, 35-43), and the curing of a deaf man (7:31-37). Far and above, the most notable of these pleas to not tell others what had taken place comes immediately after Peter's major declaration that Jesus is the Messiah as Jesus "...sternly ordered them not to tell anyone about him" (8:27-30).

As evidence of the *utilization of much of the existing material* from Mark's gospel, Matthew and Luke also record the healing of the man with leprosy verbatim as both writers reference Jesus' plea for silence (Matthew 8:1-4, Luke 5:12-14). The same can be said regarding both Matthew and Luke's versions of Peter's confession, as each writer includes Jesus' strict plea not to tell anyone (Matthew 16:13-20, Luke 9:18-22). Interestingly, Matthew chooses not to include Jesus' request for silence in his version of the healing of Jairus' daughter (9:18-19, 23-26), while Luke selects to keep it among the pages of his gospel (Luke 8:40-42, 49-56).

By the end of Matthew's gospel, the pendulum to downplay Jesus' prestige and power appears to have begun to swing to the opposite side as Jesus commands his disciples to go and "...make disciples of all nations" while teaching them "to obey everything that I have commanded you" (28:19-20). As if on cue, Luke ends his story of the healing of the Gerasene man possessed by demons by calmly noting that the man "...went away, proclaiming throughout the city how much Jesus had done for him" (8:39).

Most telling of the later gospel

> *...the pendulum to downplay Jesus' prestige and power appears to have begun to swing to the opposite side...*

writers to take advantage of the increasing opportunity to direct the narrative toward revealing Jesus as the one genuinely sent from God has to be John. More, he seems to strive to do so at every opportunity in his gospel.

The first instance of John elevating Jesus from mere messenger to mighty messiah after the opening sentences in his gospel comes as Jesus encounters the Samaritan woman at the well. Following a lengthy discussion with the woman regarding salvation and the coming Messiah, the woman ends the conversation by stating that she knows "…that the Messiah is coming…" and "When he comes, he will proclaim all things to us" (4:25). John records that Jesus then responds by saying to the woman, "…I am he…" (4:26). Also, John has Jesus speaking to the Jewish leaders that "…before Abraham, was, I am" (8:58). Following the washing of the disciples' feet, Jesus affirms the words of the disciples as they call him Lord and Teacher by stating that they "…are right, for that is what I am" (13:13). Still, John is far from concluding his efforts to capitalize on

> *…the declarations seem to follow a pattern in several instances;…*

the growing movement among the followers of Jesus for a deeper understanding of Jesus' life and teachings. In one last synchronized attempt to *pack the material* into his gospel regarding the divinity of Jesus, John introduces a series of "I Am" statements. While each of these statements seeks to indorse Jesus' consecrated position, the declarations seem to follow a pattern in several instances; namely, Jesus makes a statement of who he is and then reinforces it by performing a miracle. In the first of many of these testimonials, Jesus declares that he is "…the bread of life," which is spoken shortly after the feeding of the 5,000 (6:35, 6:1-14). The second of the "I Am" statements have Jesus proclaiming that he is "the light of the world" and comes around the time Jesus heals a blind man (8:12, 9:1-8). Around the time that he

Backfill

announces that he is "...the resurrection and the life," Jesus raises Lazarus from the dead (11:25, 11:43-44). After an exchange with Thomas over the pathway to salvation, Jesus says that he is "...the way, the truth, and the life" (14:1-6). Finally, the assertion by Jesus that he is "...the true vine..." follows his words of promise of the ongoing presence and power of the Holy Spirit in the lives of his followers (15:1, 14:26).

Equally different in the efforts of the later gospel writers to shape a narrative that strives to promote the divine side of Jesus while lessening his humanity is the explanation of events that happen to Jesus and his disciples following the resurrection.

True to form, the oldest of the gospels, the gospel of Mark, mentions three happenings in a mere nine verses, including the appearance of Jesus "...in another form..." to two of his disciples (16:12-13), the commissioning of the eleven remaining disciples even after he reprimands them for their unbelief of his resurrection (16:14-18), and the final ascension of Jesus into heaven (16:19-20).

Relatedly, Matthew chronicles his understanding of post-resurrection events with a meager nine verses which encompass the report of the guards who are bribed to say that the disciples of Jesus "...came by night and stole him away while we were sleeping," a tale that lives on even today (28:11-15), along with the commissioning of the disciples on a mountain in Galilee, in which Jesus bestows all authority to them to go forth "...and make disciples of all nations..." (16-20).

In a rather lengthy exposé of the events following Jesus' resurrection that contains nearly forty lines of scripture, Luke first notes the meeting up that Jesus has with two of his disciples along the Emmaus Road, the content of the conversation the three have as they continue their travel, the invitation for Jesus to join these two travelers at the evening

Michael F. Price

meal, and the realization of Jesus' presence at the table as he breaks the bread, which causes the eyes of the two travelers to recognize that they are in the presence of the living Lord (24:13-35). Luke follows the Emmaus Road event with a subsequent appearance of Jesus among the disciples in the city of Jerusalem in which Jesus tells them to stay in the city and evangelize (24:36-49). Luke's gospel concludes with Jesus leading his disciples out to Bethany, Jesus praying for them, followed by his ascension into heaven (24:50-53).

Far and away, the most comprehensive of the post-resurrection events appear in John's gospel. First, John writes that Jesus appears to the disciples in a house where Jesus tells the group that just as the Father has sent him, Jesus now sends them...with the blessing of the Holy Spirit (20:19-23). A week later, John records that Jesus once more appears before his disciples in the same house. This time, however, it seems that Jesus is focused on convincing a doubting Thomas that Jesus is alive by asking Thomas to touch the wounds of Jesus. When he does, Thomas not only recognizes that this is Jesus, but Thomas proudly proclaims, "My Lord and my God" (20:24-29). In the last chapter of John's gospel, Jesus first appears to seven of his disciples who are fishing on the Sea of Tiberias. Jesus then has a meal with his disciples following a record catch of one hundred fifty-three fish, followed by the plea of Jesus for Peter to feed his (Jesus) sheep. Of particular note in the concluding chapters of John's gospel is his explanation for writing the book; namely, "...so that you may come to believe that Jesus is the Messiah, the Son of God, and that through believing you may have life in his name" (20:30-31), and John's witness that the things found within this gospel are not only accurate, "but there are also many other things that Jesus did; if every one of them were written down, I suppose that the world itself could

> ...*Thomas proudly proclaims, "My Lord and my God."*

Backfill

not contain the books that would be written" (21:25).

Summary: As the years following the death and resurrection of Jesus continued to build, so too did the interest surrounding his life before the resurrection. While Mark's gospel may have supplied Jesus' followers with a general picture, it seems that the last quarter of the first century brought more profound questions. In one sense, the followers of Jesus may have wanted to know more, not only about Jesus'

> *...it seems that the last quarter of the first century brought more profound questions.*

resurrection but the people and the events that might have taken place that first Easter morning, including who came to the tomb, when did they come, and what happened after the discovery that the tomb no longer held the body of Jesus. Similarly, these same followers may have wanted to know more about the life of Jesus before his baptism since their only reference was Mark's gospel, which begins with the baptism of Jesus. It could well be that the followers of Jesus also wanted to know of the people, places, and proclamations between these two blockbuster events. It was a simple case of supply and demand. Jesus' followers demanded to know more about him, and Matthew, Luke, and John took it upon themselves to supply the information. Consequently, the timing could not have worked out any better for these later gospel writers, because they now had the last of the elements needed to backfill Mark's gospel while creating their gospel. The later gospel writers now had a *cause* and a reason to put their Christology to pen and paper, even though some of what they wrote could rightly be termed deeply biased and highly subjective.

Matthew was the first to make revisions to some of Mark's gospel. At the trailing end of his gospel, Matthew adds to the resurrection story by mentioning that an earthquake takes place on that first Easter morning. For the record, this is the second of two quakes that Matthew highlights in the course of thirty-six to forty-eight hours. The first earthquake takes place not long after Jesus takes his last breath (Matthew 27:51). Besides, Matthew redacts Mark's version of the story by including one less woman at the tomb but makes up for that by adding that there were guards and an angel. Once again, this seems to fit a pattern in Matthew's gospel, since there are no less than three angels mentioned at the beginning of his gospel. Lastly, Matthew points out that the disciples are told to go to Galilee, and Jesus will meet them there. Mark says nothing regarding this directive.

On the front-end of his gospel, Matthew seeks to enhance Mark's gospel by adding Jesus' genealogy, a visit of an angel to Joseph, the visit of the wise men, etc. In between the reproductions and the resurrections, Matthew includes several stories unique to his gospel, including the story of the healing of the two blind men, the account of the mother of James and John, and the parable of the two sons.

Several years later, Luke takes his turn at augmenting Mark's resurrection story by adding no less than two more women to the entourage on that first Easter morning, two men, no order for the disciples to go to Galilee, and no angels. Instead, Luke chooses to utilize angels on at the head of his gospel not only to tell Mary about her upcoming birth but to share with the shepherds the details surrounding the birth of Jesus. Henceforth, Luke follows the lead of Matthew by making wise use of Mark's material, but still includes several exclusive stories found only in Luke's narrative.

With minor changes, John relates his understanding of resurrection with the inclusion of two angels, more men, and fewer women and the actual appearance of Jesus at the tomb...something that Mark and Matthew mention, but Luke does not. Not to be

> *...John seems to make the birth of Jesus more of a celestial event...*

Backfill

outdone by his fellow gospel writers, John seems to make the birth of Jesus more of a celestial event as he states that there is nothing earthly about the birth of Jesus and that Jesus is God incarnate.

Each of the later gospel writers also takes a turn in the cause to transform the historical Jesus into the Risen Christ. One may never know the reasons why the Markan Jesus seeks to downplay his divinity. On the one hand, it may be connected to timing and Jesus' belief that neither the hearts of his disciples, the minds of the politicians, nor the spirit within the local religious leaders could adequately understand Jesus' mission. Maybe Jesus wanted to stay under-the-radar, and away from any political, military, or moral implications his ministry may wrongly convey along with any perceived risk his exposure might play on God's ultimate plan for him.

However, those who we know as the later gospel writers eventually came around as all three began to shape their gospels toward a narrative that presented Jesus as something more than a itinerate preacher from Nazareth. Driven by the demands of his followers to know more about Jesus and his life, Matthew, Luke, and John give the followers of Jesus what they wanted, even if that meant embellishment, inaccuracies, discrepancies, deleted texts, conflicting stories, and the advancement of a Christology that may, at times, seem established on the suspect. All told, this was genuinely backfilling at its best!

Michael F. Price

Chapter Six

Why

*"Truth is truth. Implications are subjective.
People will hear your words
and draw their own conclusion."
(Neal Shusterman, UnWholly)*

Having now uncovered how the later gospel writers went about transforming the historical Jesus into the Risen Christ, we must take a few minutes to review where we've been lest we forget.

In the first chapter, the reader was given an overview of the who, what, when, and where of each gospel, beginning with Mark's narrative, then Matthew's, Luke's, and finally, the gospel according to John. The remaining pages of the chapter centers not only on the host of commonalities these four gospels shared, including people, places, and parables, but also a brief rundown of the general differences that made each gospel unique.

The contents of chapter two began with a general definition of the term backfill, followed by a list of factors that make a successful backfill, including...

starting on the perimeter and backfilling toward the middle
utilizing much of the existing material
using small aggregate as needed
packing the material
blending-in of new material

Also contained in this chapter were several examples of the use of the five factors among the writings of the gospel writers.

Backfill

Chapter three introduced the first of three elements that the later gospel writers utilized as they went about transforming Jesus into the Risen Christ in their particular narrative. In this case, it was the element of *chronology*. For example, the reader was shown how Matthew, Luke, and John used the years between the death of Jesus and the writing of their gospel to their advantage as they build their case of an "evolving" Christ.

In chapter four, a second element used by the later gospel writers to assist in their efforts to backfill Mark's gospel was introduced. The element of *context*. The list of examples of how the gospel writers used this component includes the writers' capitalizing on the last seven words/sentences Jesus spoke from the cross.

The contents of chapter five examine the last of the elements used by the later writers to demonstrate the divinity of Jesus. Here, the aspect of *cause* is introduced. Driven mainly by the demand of the followers of Jesus to know more about his life, Matthew, Luke, and John give Jesus' followers what they want. However, their narratives are commonly filled with inaccuracies, misrepresentations, and discrepancies.

> *...we must seek to address the most pressing question of all...why.*

With the who, what, when, and where of the later gospel writers endeavors to write a new narrative on the life, teachings, death, and resurrection of Jesus behind us, we must seek to address the most pressing question of all....why? Why would the later gospel writers choose Mark as a primary source of much of the necessary information? Why is there a declining presence of the family of Jesus within the later gospels? These are just a few of the countless "why" questions that will be addressed in this section of the work. In no particular order...

> *...the element of chronology.*

Michael F. Price

Why was Jesus sent? In large part, it seems that Mark's gospel was written to strengthen the faith of those who already believed in Jesus as the Messiah and the Son of God and not so much for the new Christian. Mark's story begins with Jesus' adult baptism, and the author records no unique circumstances at his birth. The two miracles that will later form the bookends for the gospels of Matthew, Luke, and John, that is, the virgin birth and the resurrection, are nowhere to be found in Mark's original gospel. Rather than sounding as if it's a pre-ordained ministry, one senses after reading Mark's gospel that Jesus' divinity seems to unfold. Jesus "becomes" the Messiah rather than he "is" the Messiah. This may explain the countless times in Mark's gospel when Jesus pleads, and, at times, "sternly orders," others not to say a word regarding anything they had seen or experienced. It could well be that a premature discovery by others of his unique calling might bring a quicker-than-planned end to Jesus' story. The twenty-plus miracles and stories of recoveries of individuals with disease and illness are offered to give additional support to Mark's developing claim of Jesus' Messiahship.

> *...not to be served but to serve,...*

Equally evident are the human traits of his Jesus, including his cursing of the fig tree (11:12-14), the anger displayed as he cleared the temple of the moneychangers (11:15-18), his short temper upon finding the disciples asleep in Gethsemane (14:37-41), and his questioning displayed in his powerful words: "Eloi, Eloi, lama sabachthani?" (15:34). Whether he is interacting with individuals of questionable reputation, feeding 5,000 with fish and loaves, blessing little children, or watching a widow contribute her last few coins in the offering, the Markan Jesus is advancing a message that there is room in the coming kingdom for all while repentance opens the door for this gift. Mark's writing leaves no room for doubt regarding the reason

Backfill

for Jesus' presence on earth: Jesus has "...come to call not the righteous but the sinners (2:17), and "...not to be served but to serve, and to give his life as a ransom for many" (10:45).

Conversely, Matthew's gospel is an all-out effort by the writer to both connect Jesus to his Jewish heritage and to provide supplemental information about Jesus' birth, life, ministry, death, and resurrection. Thanks to Mark, who "gifts" him with an ample supply of people, parables, and proclamations to begin his work, Matthew obliges by incorporating upwards of 90% of Mark's work into his gospel. As well, Matthew seems to take advantage of the 10-15 years following the appearance of Mark's gospel to introduce his developing narrative, complete with a list of the reason Matthew feels that beckons Jesus' commission, including the declaration that Jesus "...did not come to abolish the law or the prophets...but to fulfill" (5:17), "...to the lost sheep of... Israel" (5:24, 10:6), and "...to give his life as a ransom for many" (20:28). At the same time, Matthew is quick to designate Jesus as a teacher of morals and ethics by incorporating the words of Jesus as he offered them to those who had come to hear his Sermon on the Mount (5:3-7:29). Above all, Matthew leaves no doubt that the reason for Jesus' appearance among God's creation was divinely-driven (1:18-23).

Closely following Matthew's lead, Luke also supplements Mark's reasons for Jesus' appearance by not only frontloading details surrounding Jesus' birth but also including specific stories and teachings that convey why Jesus came to: "...bring good news to the poor...claim release to the captives, and recovery of sight to the blind, to let the oppressed go free" (4:18), "...proclaim the good news of the kingdom of God..." (4:43), because "...the Son of Man came to seek out and to save the lost" (19:10).

> *...John's gospel leaves no doubt as to the widening belief that Jesus is God in the flesh.*

Michael F. Price

Far and away, one finds the culmination and fullest expression for why Jesus appears in the lives of creation to be found in the gospel of John. Beginning with the opening words which announce that Jesus has been sent to reveal God and God's glory, John seeks to bring an end to all the ambiguities and uncertainties that may have arisen within the previous gospels. In John's eyes, Jesus is the revealer of God's love for sinners (3:16), the One who will satisfy creation's deepest thirst for meaning and purpose (4:13), to do God's will (6:38), "...for judgment so that those who do not see may see..." (9:39), that people "...may have life and have it more abundantly" (10:10), all the while giving testimony to the truth of Jesus' purpose (18:37). To John, the reason why Jesus came to walk among creation is understandable. Jesus came to prove that he is the bread of life (6:35), the light of the world (8:12), the good shepherd (10:7), the resurrection and the life (11:25), the way, the truth, and the life (14:6), and the true vine by which creation is attached to God (15:1). John's gospel leaves no doubt as to the widening belief that Jesus is God in the flesh. Matthew and Luke may have reworked Mark's gospel, adding some backfill at the beginning, the middle, and the end, but John seems to have rewritten Mark's gospel. From the beginning, in the middle, and even to the end of his theological contribution, John leaves no doubt that Jesus is beyond human. Jesus is 100% divine, and his purpose was clear.

Why did the later gospel writers choose that particular time to compose their gospels? Matthew, Luke, and John may have recognized that the scarcity of evidence beyond the scriptures to authenticate events found in the scriptures could be used to their benefit. Of the countless events that are recorded to have taken place in the gospels, there is no known mention of any of these things happening among the historical records, Roman, Jewish, or otherwise. There is no record of wise men visiting Herod, Herod's edict to slaughter male

Backfill

babies under 2-years old, darkness covering the land, earthquakes, and no opening of tombs as Jesus takes his last breath, except in the gospel of Matthew. Likewise, there is no record of a governor named Quirinus declaring that males travel to Bethlehem to register, a band of angels proclaiming the birth of the Messiah to a group of shepherds, a sermon on the Mount, Jesus healing individuals of dropsy, demons, or disease, or a miraculous feeding of 5,000 people, apart from Luke's gospel. As well, there is no reference among the archives of the first century that Jesus overturned the tables of the temple moneychangers or walked on water, raised dead people or made a grand entrance to Jerusalem on that day Christians know as Good Friday, or of Jesus making an extended appearance to people after his death, except for John's writings. The silence is deafening! However, this proves to be a blessing to the later gospel writers because no one could fact-check their words. And as time went on, the written contributions of Matthew, Luke, and John further solidified any related events surrounding the life, ministry, death, and resurrection of Jesus via backfill.

> *...no one could fact-check their words.*

Why did the later gospel writers choose to use Mark's gospel as a point of reference to write their gospel? It's subjectively transparent that the later gospel writers tried to get the word out to the different Christian communities surrounding the birth, death, and resurrection of Jesus as quickly as possible. Matthew, Luke, and John may have sensed that time was of the essence, and their writing was explicitly time sensitive. To compose a new gospel meant starting from scratch, and this would only delay the circulation of their particular narrative and supposed transition of the historical Jesus to the Risen Christ. Rather than go this route, the later gospel writers cleverly used Mark's gospel as a springboard in composing their understanding of the life and ministry of Jesus. Truth be told, who wouldn't? And yet, those same later writers were more than willing to discard the portions of Mark's gospel that did not fit their efforts as they endeavored to transform the historical Jesus into the Risen Christ. Matthew supplemented Mark's gospel by adding the genealogy of Jesus, the parable of the ten bridesmaids, and the Great Commission. Among the additions Luke makes to Mark's gospel, includes seventeen parables, seven stories of miracles, and nearly one-half of Jesus' final seven words/sentences from the cross, all in hopes of forwarding a narrative of a "more divine" Jesus. With such a move, the writers could skillfully insert pieces of their Christology into Mark's gospel to give the impression that rather than theirs being a new narrative of the life of Jesus, they were simply adding "detail."

Why did the later gospel writers, beginning with Matthew and ending with John, systematically seek to incorporate less-and-less of Mark's content in their respective gospels, even though Mark's gospel may have been generally accepted among the Christian community? One possible reason why the later gospel writers included less-and-less of Mark's gospel relates to something expressed earlier in the work…simple supply and demand. Chronologically speaking, Matthew seems to be the first of the later gospel writers to respond to the growing interest to learn more about the itinerate preacher from Nazareth. In response, it appears that Matthew was more than willing to supply answers for the increasing demand to know more about Jesus, although those answers may have been highly biased, less-than-fact filled,

> *…it appears that Matthew was more than willing to supply answers for the increasing demand to know more about Jesus,…*

Backfill

and overtly subjective. A decade-or-so later, it was Luke who seemed to be more than happy to contribute responses to the developing questions bordering the events of Jesus' life, including his birth, his middle years, and the time surrounding his death and resurrection. Presumably not wanting to miss the opportunity to place his fingerprints on the life and times of Jesus, and the growing effort among the previous gospel writers (Matthew and Luke) to transform Jesus from who he "was" to who these writers believed him to "be', John seeks to seemingly address additional questions that are arising among Christian communities by further transforming the historical Jesus into the Risen Christ by including other pieces of evidence of Christ's divinity by making the birth of Jesus more of a celestial event. Responding to this growing demand to know more about the life of Jesus, the later gospel writers replied in earnest, even if this meant adding, deleting, and altering the contents of Mark's gospel with inconsistencies, inaccuracies, and biasedly-based and highly-subjective information.

Another reason for the declining presence of the content of Mark's gospel among the pages of the gospels of Matthew, Luke, and John may be related to the term "editorial privilege." Simply put: the later gospel writers wanted to place their marks on the Jesus narrative. Mark, the oldest of the gospels, chronicles one story that's not found in the later gospels...the brief, four-verse parable of the growing seed (4:26-29). In contrast, there are no less than sixteen stories, events, or miracles that are unique to the gospel of John and seem to be evenly *"layered"* among the gospels twenty-one chapters, including, the wedding feast miracle in Cana (2:1-11), Nicodemus' visit with Jesus (3:1-21), the proclamation of Jesus as the good shepherd (10:1-ff), the appearance of Jesus to a "doubting" Thomas (20:24-29), and the miraculous catch of one hundred fifty-three fish (21:1-24). Matthew lists a total of twenty-four happenings that are unique to his gospel. Most seem to appear in the second half of his narrative, including the parables of the fishing net (13:47-50), the hidden treasure (13:51-52), and the unforgiving servant (18:23-35), concise discourses on giving, prayer, and fasting (6:1-18), a lesson on divorce and celibacy (19:1-15), and the sending forth of the disciples (28:16-20). However, it is Luke who seems to make the most liberal use of including materials into his gospel that are nonexistent among the other gospels. The exclusive list of miracles, parables, and eye-opening events nearly doubles those found in John's gospel. It includes the miracle catch of fish on the lake of Gennesaret (5:1-11), the parables of the two debtors (7:41-43), the rich fool (12:16-21), and the rich man and Lazarus (16:19-31), along with the visit of Jesus to the home of Martha and Mary (10:38-42). Although the difference is minuscule, Matthew and Luke record just over twenty miracles in each of their gospels, while John relates about one-third of that number in his gospel. As for the number of parables proper to each gospel, Matthew seems to record just over twenty, while Luke chronicles around twenty-five. Remembering the "heavy-handed" borrowing that Matthew did with Mark's content, it should come as no surprise that Mark reports over twenty miracles in his gospel and nearly ten parables.

Why did the later gospel include so many of Jesus' parables in their gospels? It is clear that all four of the gospel writers not only utilized various genres in writing their gospels but did so in hopes of relating to the diversity of their audiences. Mark used a pun in his story of the healing of the demoniac Gerasene. When Jesus asked the possessed man's name, the man replied that it was Legion "…for we are many" (5:9). A pure-play on words that the man had multiple personalities. Matthew's

> *Mark used a pun in his story of the healing of the demoniac Gerasene.*

record of Jesus' words concerning adultery in which Jesus tells the crowd that if one's right eye causes one to sin, they should "...tear it out and throw it away..." can rightly be termed a hyperbole (5:29). The Magnificat, Mary's Song of Praise in Luke's gospel, is an example of poetry (1:46-55), while John's repeated use of the phrase "I am" in describing the divine position is an example of a metaphor. But if there is one form of Jesus' teaching that outweighs the presence of the other genres in the gospel, it is the type commonly known as parables. Of the nearly four dozen parables found in the gospels, upwards of one-quarter of them are shared between Matthew, Mark, and Luke, including the parable(s) of the old clothing patch and the new wineskins (Matthew 9:16-17, Mark 2:21-22, Luke 5:36-39), the parable regarding the light under a shade (Matthew 5:14-16, Mark 4:21-22, Luke 8:16), and the parable of the mustard seed (Matthew 13:31-32, Mark 4:30-32, Luke 13:18-19). As further proof of Jesus' widespread use of parables as a teaching tool in his ministry, Mark mentions one parable, the parable of the seed, a parable that's absent from both Matthew and Luke's gospels (4:26-29). As for Matthew, he includes nearly a dozen parables in his gospel that are not documented in either Mark or Luke's gospels, including the parable of the treasure hidden in the field (13:44). Regarding Luke's gospel, there are nearly twenty parables that are unique to his gospel and absent from the gospels of Matthew and Mark, including the parable of the great dinner (14:7-11). There are no parables in the gospel of John as much of his stories could be termed allegories and not parables, because parables seek to teach a moral or religious lesson. In contrast, the lesson that arises from an allegory is mostly left up to the interpretation of the listener. When asked by his disciples why he used parables in his teaching, Jesus responds by implying that his purpose seems to be to both

> *...reveal to the believer and to conceal from the nonbelievers.*

reveal to the believer and to conceal from nonbelievers (13:10-13). Using the everyday language of craftsmen, artisans, and laborers, and presented simplistically so that the point of the parable could not only be understood but easily remembered, the topic of Jesus' parables is commonly focused on things that those in the crowd could relate to, such as farming, fishing, or families. One must remember, however, that underneath the plain language and simple truth of the parables commonly lie a more profound meaning on themes such as redemption (Luke 15:11-32), forgiveness (Luke 7:36-50), the coming kingdom (Matthew 25:1-13), and love (Mark 12:1-11).

Why do the later gospel writers seem to increase the power and prestige of Jesus in their gospels while decreasing the relevance of those around Jesus? It could be that fear of the possibility of a Jesus (family) empire laid heavy on the hearts and minds of the later gospel writers. More than once in his gospel, Mark states that Jesus had not only brothers but also sisters. Mark supplies the names of the brothers of Jesus later in his gospel as James, Joses, Judas, and Simon, while the names of the sisters go unnamed. Matthew acknowledges Mark's claim for Jesus having brothers but initially mentions no sisters. Several verses later in his gospel, however, Matthew does list the names of Jesus' brothers, although Matthew spells one of the brother's name as Joses for Joseph and lists Simon before Judas. Further, Matthew acknowledges in that same chapter that Jesus does have female siblings. If Mary was a virgin before Jesus' birth and his brothers and sisters were born after him, this possibly makes Jesus the oldest of the children, and perhaps James, the second oldest, then Joses/Joseph, followed by the remaining two brothers. However, the legend of the scriptures seems to imply that Jesus was Mary's one-and-only child. Subsequently, the siblings of Jesus mentioned in Mark and Matthew maybe

Backfill

Joseph's children from a prior marriage. By the time of Luke's writing (circa 75-90CE), the names of the brothers are nowhere to be found among the pages of Luke's gospel, and there is no mention whatsoever of Jesus having sisters. The same goes for John's gospel. Could the reason behind the shrinking presence of Jesus' siblings, especially his brothers, among the pages of the gospels of Matthew, Luke, and John, be traced to fear among the writers of the possibility of a Jesus dynasty? It could be that this second generation of Christians, which most likely includes the later gospel writers, envisioned a non-stop line of the relatives of Jesus as heads of the movement. In the minds of the later gospel writers, a likely avenue to put an end to this succession was to slowly decrease the importance of the siblings of Jesus by reducing their presence in the gospels.

Why is there such an increasingly disparaging treatment of Judas among the words of the gospel writers, especially the later gospel writers? The Judas narrative is found in all four gospels, with varying degrees of information and condemnation. However, he is increasingly exposed among the later gospel writers as being the most despicable among the disciples of Jesus. As the oldest of the gospels, Mark is the first of the gospel writers to introduce Judas. Here, Mark lists Judas last among the twelve disciples with a damning phrase following Judas' name that reads, "…who betrayed him" (3:19). He is not mentioned again in Mark's gospel until well into the passion narrative, which begins in chapter eleven and ends with chapter sixteen. The bulk of Judas' involvement is concentrated in chapter fourteen. Following a difference among the disciples that centers around a discussion whether an ointment brought by a woman to anoint Jesus was a wise use of money, Mark records that Judas approaches the chief priest with an intent "…to betray him (Jesus) to them." After agreeing to a sum of money to give Judas for his intentions, the plot to betray Jesus begins in earnest (14:3-11). As he is concluding a time of prayer in the Garden of Gethsemane, Mark writes that Judas appears with a crowd who are brandishing weapons. Referring to him now as "the betrayer" (14:44), Judas tells the leaders of the raucous crowd that the one he (Judas) kisses is Jesus. Upon kissing Jesus and referring to him as "rabbi" (14:45), Jesus is promptly arrested. From there, one hears no more of Judas in Mark's gospel.

A decade or so later, as he is composing his gospel, Matthew adds some details to Mark's understanding of the Judas narrative. Following the lead of Mark, Matthew first lists Judas among the original disciples. True to form, Judas is not only listed last among the twelve but with a post-script that reads "…the one who betrayed him (Jesus)" (10:4). Judas does not show up again in Matthew's gospel until the concluding chapters of the gospel. *Packing with some new material*, Matthew records the events of Judas' betrayal in this manner. First, Matthew has Judas asking the chief priests for compensation for his efforts to betray Jesus. The agreed-upon amount is thirty pieces of silver. With this, the plan to betray Jesus is set in motion. Following

> ***Packing with some new material…***

a time of prayer in Gethsemane, Matthew has Jesus commenting to his disciples that his (Jesus) time for death is nearing because the betrayer of Jesus "…is at hand" (26:46). As the crowd arrives, chief priests and elders alike, Judas not only kisses Jesus but calls him rabbi. Responding, Jesus says to Judas for him to do what he came to do. From there, Jesus is arrested and taken first to Caiaphas, the high priest, and then to Pilate. Upon hearing that Pilate has condemned Jesus to death, Matthew records that Judas not only repents for his scornful act but seeks to return the thirty pieces of silver by terming the silver as "blood money" for an innocent man. The chief priests and scribes decline the silver. After throwing down the silver at the feet of the chief priests, scribes, and

Backfill

elders, Matthew notes that Judas then goes and hangs himself. Matthew concludes his narrative of Judas' actions by adding that the chief priests and scribes decide to accept the silver and buy a field in which foreigners will be buried. All this to fulfill what the prophet had said centuries earlier regarding the purchase of a potter's field (27:3-10).

As for Luke and his gospel written anywhere between ten and twenty-five years after Mark's gospel, he, also, first introduces Judas as one of the twelve original disciples and the last of the disciples listed. However, Luke is quick to point out that Judas, the son of James, is a different Judas from the one "…who became a traitor" (6:16). Frontloading both Mark and Matthew's version of the Judas narrative, Luke adds additional details. First, Luke incorporates that it is the Feast of Unleavened Bread (Passover), and it was the chief priest and scribes that initially set the plan into action. After Satan enters him, Judas approaches the religious leaders about his inclusion in the plan to have Jesus put to death. After agreeing to payment, Luke writes that Judas then begins looking for the right opportunity to betray Jesus. Recognizing the plan, Jesus seems to call-out Judas as Jesus and his disciples gather for the Last Supper. Following the blessing and breaking of bread and the sharing of the cup, Jesus speaks, saying, "…the one who betrays me is with me, and his hand is on the table…" but he quickly adds "…woe to that one by whom he is betrayed!" (22:22). Luke's gospel is void of any further references to Judas.

At just about the same place in his gospel that Luke first mentions Judas, the last of the later gospel writers, John, introduces the reader to Judas. As expected, John seems to follow the lead of his contemporaries by offering a less-than-glowing view of the actions of Judas. Saying that one of the twelve is a devil, John is quick to note that Jesus is "…speaking of Judas

> **…*John seems to "heap gas on the fire"…***

son of Simon Iscariot, for he, though one of the twelve, was going to betray him" (6:70-71). From there, John seems to "heap gas on the fire" on what the previous three writers have said about Judas. First, John mentions Judas' objection to Mary's anointing the feet of Jesus by Judas' stern conviction that the money that was used to purchase the perfume could have been given to the poor. Bracketed and seeming to insert his opinion for why Judas would say such a thing, John writes that Judas did not care about the poor, but because Judas was a thief and would commonly use his position as the treasurer of the group to steal money from the group (12:4-6). Next, John reports that during the washing of the feet of the disciples just before the Passover, a time when the devil has already invaded the heart of Judas, Jesus tells his followers that servants are not greater than their masters, adding that Jesus is not speaking of all of the disciples, but by implication, "…the one who ate my bread…" and "…has lifted his heel against me" (13:18). Judas surfaces for a third time in John's gospel as Jesus and the disciples gather for a Passover meal. Sharing with the disciples that one of them will betray him, the disciples want to know who among the twelve would do such a thing. Jesus responds, "It is the one to whom I give this piece of bread when I have dipped it in the dish. So when he had dipped the piece of bread, he gave it to Judas son of Simon Iscariot. After he had received the bread, Satan entered into him. Jesus said to him, do quickly what you are going to do" (13:26-27). John offers an added opinion that seems to add confusion regarding the words of Jesus. As the group's treasurer, the disciples believed that Jesus was telling Judas to either go and buy some things the groups needs to celebrate the festival, or that Judas should give the money to the poor (13:29). A fourth and final mention of Judas in John's gospel occurs most likely in the Garden of Gethsemane. However, the garden's proper name is not explicitly mentioned. Along with a group of soldiers, police from the chief priests, and some

Backfill

Pharisees, the group approaches Jesus with lanterns and weapons. Asking who they are looking for, Jesus is told the man from Nazareth. More than once, Jesus answers that he is the one. John records that Judas says nothing during this midnight encounter, but stands idly nearby (18:1-5). Thus ends John's record of the Judas narrative in the fourth gospel.

Although Matthew lists no less than eight references to Judas in his gospel, far and away, it is John who makes the most citations to Judas...ten times...and the vast majority are pejorative. The number is double the times that Judas is mentioned in such a critical fashion in Luke's gospel and nearly three times more than Mark mentions Judas in his gospel. Still, it would be difficult to ascertain why the later gospels writers would feel such outright disdain for Judas. Any attempt to explain the scorn felt by Matthew, Luke, or John would not only be pure conjecture but lie outside the contents of the gospels. Nevertheless, the disparaging remarks originating with Mark, increasing with Matthew and Luke, and culminating with John, causes one to speculate why the mounting attack.

> *...it would be difficult to ascertain why the later gospel writers would feel such disdain for Judas.*

Ethically speaking, can one rightfully blame Judas for being so money conscious that he takes offense for the purchase of perfume over the needs of the poor? Is it because Judas is the only non-Galilean of the twelve disciples that Matthew seems to set all this anti-Judas rhetoric in motion? Does it make sense that Matthew all but singles out Judas as his betrayer at the Last Supper, but later Jesus calls Judas "friend"? Why is Matthew the only one of the gospel writers to mention the circumstances behind Judas ending his life, and what, if any, did this add to the story? Why is it necessary for John to note that Satan entered Judas not once but twice (13:2, 13:27)? In like manner, why does John find it necessary to add his opinion as if John knows what's really on the heart of Judas (12:6)? Above all, why was it essential for the later gospel writers to imply that Judas was more concerned about the bottom line on his ledger than the life of the Lord? Remember, Mark does not mention Judas as being present at the Last Supper, possessed by Satan, or being a thief. Instead, one may even go as far as say that Jesus was not the only one sacrificed in the gospels. And in their intentional way, it was through the efforts that the later gospel writers made it happen! If not for the direct, overt, and manipulative actions of Matthew, Luke, and John to transform the historical Jesus into the Risen Christ, who knows if Judas may have lived long enough to take his place among the ranks the likes of Peter, James, and the other disciples.

On the surface, it seems that there is absolutely no need for a betrayer in the gospels. Jesus could have been arrested any number of times because it would have been simple to keep tabs on his whereabouts. The religious authorities did not need a betrayal, only the gospel writers so that a few more "prophecies" could bear out.

Why were the later gospel writers so detailed in some parts of their respective gospels and so wobbly with details in other parts? Among the stories that are found in all four gospels is the triumphal entry of Jesus into the holy city on that day Christians have termed Palm Sunday. As expected, there are different variations between the respective gospels.

Mark writes that as Jesus and his disciples are nearing Jerusalem, at Bethpage and Bethany, near the Mount of Olives, Jesus sends two of his disciples into the village. There, Jesus tells the two that they will find a colt that has never been ridden. Should

> **Among the stories that are found in all four gospels is the triumphal entry of Jesus into the holy city...**

someone ask the disciples why the colt is needed, the disciples are to simply say that the Lord needs it, and the colt will be returned shortly. When the two disciples hit town, they find a colt, but when asked by a person who sees them untying the colt asks what gives, the disciples tell the person that the Lord needs it. Upon returning to Jesus, cloaks are thrown on the colt, and Jesus gets on the animal. As Jesus makes his way toward Jerusalem, people along the road begin to spread cloaks and tree branches ahead of Jesus. Also, some went ahead of Jesus, who were shouting, "Hosanna! Blessed is the one who comes in the name of the Lord! Blessed is the coming kingdom of our ancestor David! Hosanna in the highest heaven!" (11:1-10).

Matthew records the event with some modifications. When the group was near Jerusalem, at Bethpage, Jesus sends two disciples ahead with some specific instructions. In the town, they will find a donkey that is tied up along with her colt nearby. They are to untie the two animals and bring them to Jesus. If someone says something, the two disciples are to simply reply that the Lord needs them, and the two animals will be returned shortly. All this was to fulfill what had been spoken through the prophet. Upon returning with the animals, cloaks are placed on both the animals and Jesus "…sat on them" (21:7). In addition to spreading their cloaks on the road along with tree branches, those that went ahead and those that followed were shouting "Hosanna to the Son of David, Blessed is the one who comes in the name of the Lord! Hosanna in the highest heaven" (21:1-9).

As for Luke, he chronicles things this way in his gospel (19:29-40). As Jesus and his disciples near Bethpage and Bethany, at the Mount of Olives, Jesus sends two of his disciples ahead. There, the two will find a colt that has never been ridden. The two disciples are to untie the colt and bring it to Jesus. If the two are asked why the colt is being untied and taken away, the disciples are to respond that the Lord needs it. As the two disciples are untying the colt and taking it away, they are asked why by the colt's owner. The response of the disciples is enough to satisfy the owner's curiosity. Upon returning to Jesus, cloaks are placed on the colt, Jesus then takes his place on the colt, and begins his ride toward Jerusalem. Those along the way spread their cloaks on the road as Jesus approaches. As the processional approaches the Mount of Olives, the "...whole multitude of the disciples began to praise God joyfully with a loud voice for all the deeds they had seen..." (19:37). The voices were saying, "Blessed is the king who comes in the name of the Lord! Peace in heaven, and glory in the highest heaven!" (19:29). Luke adds that the Pharisees in the crowd order Jesus to have his disciples stop what they're doing, to which Jesus replies, "...if these were silent, the stones would shout out" (19:40).

Lastly, John reports things this way on that first Palm Sunday. As the crowds gathered for the (Passover) festival, the word began to circulate that Jesus was coming to Jerusalem. Cutting palm branches, the crowd went out to meet Jesus, shouting, "Hosanna! Blessed is the one who comes in the name of the Lord-the King of Israel!" (12:13). Finding a young donkey, Jesus sits on it, according to a proclamation: "Do not be afraid, daughter of Zion. Look, your king is coming, sitting on a donkey's colt" (12:15). While the disciples did not initially understand these things, they then remembered all that had been written of him (Jesus) and been done to him. Moreover, the crowd that had been with Jesus when he raised Lazarus from the dead went out to meet Jesus. Seeing all of this, the Pharisees in the crowd comment to one another, saying, "You see, you can do nothing. Look, the world has gone after him!" (12:12-19).

On the surface, there are several commonalities among the various descriptions of what happened that epic day. First, it seems that two of the three later gospel writers follow the lead of Mark and put the location of the events near Bethpage and the Mount of Olives. In like manner, both Matthew and Luke agree with Mark that Jesus sends two of his disciples into the town with strict orders, although the disciples are unnamed. Similarly, Mark, Matthew, and Luke all record that the disciples should expect someone asking them about them taking the animal(s). Subsequently, the disciples are to respond by replying that the Lord needs it. Albeit in different places during the processional and in different verbiage, all three gospel writers, Mark, Matthew, and Luke, convey that those in the crowd not only laid cloaks on the back(s) of the animal that Jesus was riding on but also on the road. Finally, all four writers note that there were shouts of acclamation coming from the crowd as Jesus passed by.

Conversely, John says nothing in his gospel about the location as being neither Bethpage nor the Mount of Olives, nothing about disciples, and nothing about cloaks. From there, the diversity of details of what went on that day, who was in the crowd, and what was said are numerous.

> *...the diversity of what went on that day, who was in the crowd, and what was said are numerous.*

Mark records that the colt the disciples are to bring back is one that "...no one has ever sat" (11:2). As he details the events surrounding Jesus' entry into Jerusalem, one first notices from Matthew's account that he maintains his theme that Jesus is the Jewish Messiah by not only noting that this event is in keeping with the words of the prophet, but the words are also coming from the crowd (21:5, 9). Most striking, Matthew mentions two animals, "...a donkey tied, and a colt with her..." (21:2). After bringing "...them..." to Jesus, cloaks are placed on "...them..." and "...Jesus sat on them" (21:6-7). As one contrasts the words of Mark with those of Matthew, one must ask if they're one or two animals? If there were two animals, as Matthew writes in his gospel, how did

Michael F. Price

Jesus sit on two animals?

Seeking to share more details regarding Jesus' entry into Jerusalem, Luke first notes the presence of the owners of the colt, as in more than one owner (19:33). Next, Luke mentions a "...path down from the Mount of Olives..." along with a "...whole multitude of the disciples..." who were praising God (19:37). Lastly, there is mention in the third gospel of Pharisees who are among the crowd and their plea for Jesus to have the disciples stop the celebrating (19:39-40).

Finally, it is John's turn to place his "slant" on the events of that first Palm Sunday. In contrast, John is precise that branches that the crowd laid on the road are the "...branches of palm trees..." and the crowd left Jerusalem and "...went out to meet him" (12:13). Among those in the crowd, John writes, are a group of Pharisees who seem helpless to do anything. Above all, John notes that the disciples did not understand what was happening. It was only later that the disciples "...remembered that these things had been written and had been done to him" (12:16).

While the efforts of the gospel writers seem to be directed at creating a degree of harmony by *blending* gospels, their labors at providing details only further muddy the waters. Was there only one owner of the animals or more than one? Were the events of that day to fulfill an earlier directive voiced by an unnamed prophet? Were the crowds that lined the road that day part of the Jesus entourage coming *to* Jerusalem, or were the crowds coming *from* the holy city? It is only after the Jerusalem crowd seeks clarity to the identity of Jesus; they are enlightened. Who first took control of the animal? Was it the two, unnamed disciples, or was it Jesus who "...found a young donkey and sat on it..." as John says? From where did the

> **...the gospel writers appear to be somewhat loose about their understanding of the facts surrounding the life of Jesus.**

Backfill

disciples "read" of these things that had been "written" about Jesus' entry into Jerusalem?

On the contrary, it seems there are times when the gospel writers appear to be somewhat loose about their understanding of the facts surrounding the life of Jesus. Although they are minor in the eyes of many, these incidents lend further proof of the later gospel writers to shape a narrative to their Christology.

As they prepare to carry out their mission, Mark writes that Jesus tells the disciples to take nothing "...except a staff; no bread, no bag, no money in their belts; but to wear sandals and not to put on two tunics" (6:8-9). Matthew notes that Jesus tells the disciples that they are to "Take no gold, or silver, or copper, in your belts, no bag for your journey, or two tunics, or sandals, or a staff..." (10:9-10). To finish, Luke has Jesus telling his disciples to "Take nothing for your journey, no staff, nor bag, nor bread, nor money-not even an extra tunic" (9:3). Once again, the efforts of the writers to add detail to their gospel does nothing but add confusion. Are the disciples to take a staff with them or not? What about sandals? Can they take anything?

Luke records in his gospel that while he is being beaten and mocked by the guards, Jesus is blindfolded (22:64). The other gospel writers say nothing about this whatsoever.

In the feeding of the 4,000, why do Matthew and Mark allude to the questioning by the disciples of how Jesus will feed the crowd when Jesus fed a 20% larger group and with less food earlier in their respective gospels? Was it merely a lack of memory on the part of the disciples, or were the two writers seeking to further capitalize on the disciples' lack of faith in Jesus?

In John's gospel, Jesus claims that Moses wrote about him, but no passage is cited (5:46). Further, why did Jesus choose a devil

> *...why did Jesus choose a devil (Judas) as one of his disciples?*

Michael F. Price

(Judas) as one of his disciples (6:70)?

Further confirmation that the relaxed efforts of the later gospel writers resulted in confusion and uncertainty is shown in countless texts, including, Matthew's prophetic attribution to Jeremiah when, in fact, the words actually comes from the prophet Zechariah (27:9), the confusion over the Lord's Prayer (Matthew uses debts, and the prayer as being part of the broader discourse known as the Sermon on the Mount, while Luke uses sins and records that the request for Jesus to teach the disciples to pray in the same manner as John the Baptist taught his followers, Matthew 6:9-13, Luke 11:1-4), the healing of Peter's mother-in-law (Mark records that the healing takes place in the house of Simon and Andrew, with James and John present, and that Jesus took the woman by the hand and lifted her up (1:29-31); Matthew writes that the miracle takes place at Peter's house as Jesus simply touches the woman's hand (8:14-15); while Luke reports that it was Simon's house and Jesus returned the woman to new life by simply standing over her (Luke 4:38-39); and the diverse reporting of Mark, Matthew, and Luke surrounding the story of Bartimaeus (Mark implies the event takes place near Jericho and involves an individual, a blind beggar named Bartimaeus; Matthew chronicles that Jesus was leaving Jericho when he encounters two blind men and no mention of the names or why these men are along the road; while Luke seems to form a composite of Mark and Matthew's stories by writing that it was a solitary, and blind, beggar with no name (Mark 10:46-52, Matthew 20:29-34, and Luke 18:35-43).

And speaking of the Sermon on the Mount, Matthew records that Jesus says to the crowd, "Blessed are the poor in spirit" (Mt 5:3). In later words, Matthew writes that Jesus says, "Blessed are those who hunger and thirst for righteousness, for they will be filled" (5:6). Conversely, Luke writes in his gospel that the words of Jesus are more like "Blessed are you who are poor" (6:20) and "Blessed are you who are hungry

Backfill

now, for you will be filled" (6:21). One might say that the differences in detail are relevant and fit the agendas of each writer since Matthew has Jesus going up the mountain (5:1); hence, the Sermon on the Mount, and Luke, in a more compact narrative, has Jesus coming down from the mountain "...and stood on a level plain,..." (6:17).

> ...*the differences in detail are relevant and fit the agendas of each writer*...

Overall, it seems that the gospel writers, especially the later ones, Matthew, Luke, and John, often showed their "eye" for detail by adding things that are absent or missing from other gospels. This is particularly true when the writers felt the inclusion would possibly add veracity or authenticity to their narrative. Why else would John specify that it was "palm" branches that were laid along the road as Jesus made his way into Jerusalem and not just "cut" and "leafy" branches as Matthew and Mark record? Besides, the gospel writers may have believed that the add-ons somehow "spiced up" the texts and was a way of displaying the writer's creativity, writing skills, and attention to detail.

On the other hand, one might say as an example that John's efforts at enhancing the story by either adding or intentionally deleting certain things did nothing but add confusion to the overall event. More problematic, however, may be the symbolic value of the numbers cited explicitly in some of John's texts...the Samaritan woman's five husbands (4:10), the invalid's thirty-eight-year illness (5:5), and a catch of 153 fish (21:11). Including such specific numbers may wrongly lead one to believe that these are not chance numbers, but accurate and truthful ones. Subsequently, this causes a person to wonder which version of an event is the more genuine one? Is the loose inclusion of specific details in a story, yet absent from the other gospels, enough to bring the details and the story into question? In this case, the energies and creativity of

Michael F. Price

the gospel writers may have worked not only to the detriment of a particular writer but quite possibly to the acceptance of other passages in the writer's gospel.

Why did the later gospel writers include all the inconsistencies, misinformation, and discrepancies in their gospels if they sensed their inclusions might not be legitimate? Generally speaking, one could say that the later gospel writers may not have been fully aware of the discrepancies and misinformation in their gospels, since the names, places, and proclamations were coming from sources that were years, possibly decades, removed from the actual time when events happened. It was after one compares-and-contrasts the content of a particular gospel with another gospel would the differences become noticeable. Consider the question of how many women showed up at the tomb of Jesus that first Easter morning? John says there was 1…Matthew writes there are 2…Mark records 3…Luke relates that there at least 4. How many words/sentences did Jesus say from the cross? The oldest of the gospels (Mark) indicates that Jesus spoke one sentence, and the same goes for Matthew's account. Luke and John both record that Jesus says it's more like three sentences. If John the Baptist was baptizing individuals in the Jordan River as a sign of forgiveness, why did Jesus come to be baptized? What had he done that he was asking to be cleansed and forgiven? Why does Joseph drag along his pregnant wife of nine months with him to Bethlehem when it was only he that had to go there?

Matthew may not have been aware of the dissimilarities between his version of the feeding of the 5,000 and Luke's account, if not for the appearance of Luke's gospel a decade later.

> *…the later gospel writers produced a narrative about the life of Jesus that will go unchanged indefinitely.*

Backfill

Similarly, Luke may not have been aware of the overt distinctions between his narrative of the resurrection and John's storyline, if John's gospel had never appeared in the lives of first-century Christians. This may explain why the titles to each gospel are termed "The Gospel According to…" On the other hand, since Matthew borrowed extensively from Mark's gospel and Luke the same to a lesser degree, and John may have known or had access to the contents of all three gospels as he was composing his gospel, it could be that the writers were more concerned with distribution than discrepancies, more with the message than mistakes, and more with circulation than consistency. Right or wrong, fact or fantasy, intentional or unintentional, the later gospel writers produced a narrative about the life of Jesus that will go unchanged indefinitely. While they may not have planned it, the chances of their work being altered or modified are unlikely, and the product of their work is here to stay. It may be that each gospel writer was under the impression that their narrative would be read as a singular piece of literature and not as part of a series, and it was only after the last of the gospels came out that the discrepancies began to surface! Whatever the case, the gospel writers have produced narratives that are nothing less than a one-way street, and any chance of correcting the inconsistencies, discrepancies, or misinformation will likely find a significant challenge. As Judge Marilyn Milian of the Peoples Court so aptly puts it, "say it, forget it; write it, regret it."

Michael F. Price

Chapter Seven

*"If a window of opportunity appears,
don't pull down the shades."*
(Tom Peters)

In the legal world, the three most important words could well be *motive*, *means*, and *opportunity*. As waypoints, *motive* translates into the reason or the desire to do something. In other terms, motive equates into why. Equally important is the *means*, because it helps to clarify how things took place. The third factor in the triangle is *opportunity*, and it focuses on the element of availability or presence. Upon reviewing the previous pages, it becomes clear that these three elements were seemingly present as the later gospel writers known to Christians as Matthew, Luke, and John, intentionally sought to recast the historical Jesus into the Risen Christ.

> *...Matthew, Luke, and John, intentionally sought to recast the historical Jesus into the Risen Christ.*

First, it could be that Matthew, Luke, and John, had a transparent *motive* in composing their respective gospels. The purpose was to present Jesus as something more than an itinerate preacher from a small village in northern Galilee named Nazareth. Utilizing the contents of Mark's gospel as a foundation, Matthew, Luke, and John began their efforts on the *perimeter* of the life of Jesus...his death and birth...and work toward the middle, adding, deleting, and modifying the stories from Mark to shape and mold their specific gospel. Matthew and Luke take the seemingly possible reality of Mark's gospel that Jesus is the son of God, backfilling as they go, and *layer* Mark's gospel with new stories of divine proclamations, of diseased and infirmed individuals being healed, and countless lessons of love, acceptance, and the coming kingdom via hyperboles, metaphors, and parables.

To fulfill his theology that Jesus is the long-awaited Messiah of the Jewish people, Matthew shapes his gospel in such a way that the prophets of the Old Testament seemed to predict his birth, including where he would be born, things that Jesus did during his ministry, even to the point of Jesus speaking words from the cross that reference a passage from the Book of Psalms.

In like manner, Luke seems to follow the lead of his contemporary by frontloading Matthew's version of the birth of Jesus by adding an angelic proclamation to shepherds, supplementing Matthew by adding several more stories of healing and resuscitation, and even a "new and detailed" understanding of the events of that first Easter morning. Luke also goes as far as to declare in the early pages of his gospel his motive, namely, "...to write an orderly account..." (1:1-3).

> *...John takes the seemingly possible reality of Jesus' divinity in Mark, along with the high probability of the divinity of Matthew and Luke's Jesus, to the certainty that Jesus is God incarnate.*

Writing nearly two decades after the appearance of Matthew (circa 75-85CE) and Luke's gospels (circa 75-90), as much as four decades following the advent of Mark's gospel (circa 65-75CE), and a full half-century or more after the death and resurrection of Jesus, John takes the seemingly possible reality of Jesus' divinity in Mark, along with the high probability of the divinity of Matthew and Luke's Jesus, to the certainty that Jesus is God incarnate. More, there is little doubt that the last of the gospel writers did not believe that Jesus was the Logos, and his presentation of seven "I am's" of Jesus stands as one of many proofs.

Michael F. Price

Despite their concerted efforts, at times, it is difficult to ascertain fact from fiction, legend from truth, fabrication from fidelity. And each time some of the stories appeared, it's evident that some embellishment had knowingly taken place. In most cases, it seems the writers made little, if any, attempt to determine the legitimacy of what they were recording. Some of these "trimmings" were small ones and discreet to most readers; other adjustments are more conspicuous; while still other changes by the later gospel writers to Mark's content is quite clear. Matthew, Luke, and John added material that was in Mark's gospel to lend support to their developing Christology. Clearly, the later gospel writers were more than happy to use what Mark had given them as starting material. One would be crazy not to utilize such a valuable and generally accepted source. And yet, Matthew, Luke, and John seemed to be just as willing to discard portions of Mark's gospel if it did not fit their efforts at transforming the historical Jesus into the Risen Christ. If what Mark provided was beneficial to their endeavor, the later gospel writers made full use of it. If a particular piece of Mark's gospel did not help, Matthew, Luke, and John, simply reworked or re-tired that section. It's not as if these later gospel writers had little regard or value of Mark's work; they did, or else they would not have used Mark's content as foundational material in their gospels. Still, these same three writers were canny enough to realize that they could use some of Mark's gospel to gain a degree of respectability from their readers. It seems that the goal of the later gospel writers went beyond the simple preservation of the details of Jesus' life or to forward his teachings. Equally, if not more, significant to Matthew, Luke, and John was their endeavor to convey

> *...it's difficult to imagine that the later gospel writers did not recognize the power of their pen to control the future theological narrative...*

Backfill

Jesus as a fresh and innovative way to demonstrate God's presence in the lives of creation.

Bottom line: it's difficult to imagine that the later gospel writers did not recognize the power of their pen to control the future theological narrative and understanding of the birth, life, teaching, death, and resurrection of Jesus. Once these three writers recognized this formidable and useful tool, the gloves came off, and the freedom of their written word abounded.

If the motive of Matthew, Luke, and John was to transform Jesus from itinerate preacher to the Risen Christ, these three writers most certainly had the *means* to assist them in their efforts. The size of Mark's gospel, a short fifteen chapters, and less than seven hundred verses, seemed to invite the later gospel writers to add to Mark's content, and they did! Although he copied nearly 90% of Mark's content and placed it in his gospel, Matthew still felt it necessary to supplement Mark's gospel as needed. The result is that Matthew intentionally lengthens Mark's gospels by nearly 75% by adding fifty percent more verses and over sixty percent more verbiage. Whereas Mark begins his gospel with the baptism of Jesus, Matthew commences his gospel by presenting the genealogy of Jesus, and the proclamation that Jesus is the Messiah. Matthew follows by adding an account of Jesus' birth, the Sermon on the Mount, and more detail to the passion narrative by including the tearing of the curtain temple, an earthquake, and resurrection of the saints.

Recognizing the same chance to supplement Mark's gospel to further his cause but still utilizing Mark's basic outline, Luke increases the volume of Mark's gospel by nearly two-thirds by adding eight additional chapters, almost five hundred more verses and increasing the total number of words from nearly nine hundred to practically twelve hundred. The additions to Mark's gospel by the third of the gospel writers include no less than fifteen new parables, more than five miracles not found in either Mark or Matthew, and added detail of the resurrection story.

However, the last of the gospel writers, John, does not seem to take advantage of the brevity of Mark's gospel as Matthew and Luke did. Instead, John appears to choose quality over quantity by using only two hundred more words than Mark in his gospel. The inclusion of the "I am" statements, the story of the Logos, and the story of the woman at the well all convey the message that John wants to make every word in his gospel have meaning and relevance to his belief that Jesus is truly God in the flesh.

Without a doubt, the later gospel writers had the means to construct a new narrative. Not only did they have the availability of Mark's gospel, but Matthew, Luke, and John had 100% control of the content that went into their gospels and how that content would be arranged. Subsequently, these later gospel writers may have viewed themselves as more than merely editors or compilers who passed on what they had heard without comment. They took an active role in attempting to introduce the teachings and stories of Jesus to a certain context, for a certain purpose, and for a certain audience. These three later gospel writers used just enough of Mark's gospel to sound harmonious, but still left themselves enough elbowroom to make the content of their gospel plausible and not seem too far to the left. It was they who held the reigns of what was being produced and distributed and not editors, publishers, or even proof-readers...and they knew it!

> *These three later gospel writers used just enough of Mark's gospel to sound harmonious, but still left themselves enough elbowroom to make the content of their gospel plausible...*

Above all, Matthew, Luke, and John had an abundance of *opportunities* to achieve their goal of directing the Jesus narrative. At one end, these three writers had *chronology*

Backfill

(time) working for them. Each writer seems to take full benefit of the years between Jesus' birth and the appearance of their respective gospels to free themselves from being "fact-checked" by relatives of Jesus, his disciples, or anybody else. One must remember that it was nearly three-quarters of a century between the birth of Jesus and the writing of Mark's gospel, another decade or so until the appearance of the gospels of Matthew and Luke, and as much as a full century until the birth of John's gospel. Knowing that there was simply no one alive at the time these later gospel writers are doing their thing to challenge their understanding of people, places, or proclamations, provided not only a sense of literary independence but also it translated into an unencumbered track for Matthew, Luke, and John to pursue their developing Christology.

Similarly, the later gospel writers were keen to a mounting interest for a deeper understanding of Jesus' life and teachings, elements seemingly absent in Mark's gospel. In response, it appears that Matthew was more than willing to be the first in the *cause* to supply answers for the increasing demand to know more about Jesus, even though those answers are highly biased, less-than-fact filled, and overtly subjective.

In due time, Luke takes his turn at addressing the questions that have surfaced regarding Jesus' life. *Utilizing much of the existing material* found in Mark's gospel but not afraid to include *small pieces to create better backfill*, Luke seeks to deepen the understanding of the unique traits of Jesus that Mark and Matthew may have overlooked while also adding his own perspective on the divinity of Jesus. Not to be outdone by his fellow gospel

> *...Matthew, Luke, and John find themselves in the perfect context to not only do their thing but to compose a gospel that frees them of any type of consequences, constraints, or retribution...social, religious, or political.*

95

writers, John takes a personal swipe at supplying answers to the questions surrounding Jesus' birth, life, and resurrection. Driven by the demands of his followers to know more about Jesus and his life, Matthew, Luke, and John give the followers of Jesus what they wanted.

And in the middle of the opportunity to direct a narrative toward a more divine Jesus, Matthew, Luke, and John find themselves in the perfect *context* to not only do their thing but to compose a gospel that frees them of any type of consequences, constraints, or retribution...social, political, or religious. The lack of any kind of control not only opened the door for these three later writers but offered them a free pass to embellish, manipulate, and alter events and people into a mosaic of their liking. Matthew, Luke, and John had a blank page and utilized this context to their benefit.

Probable to possible to positive...this seems to describe the roller coaster ride that the gospel writers take us on as it relates to the divinity of Jesus. Several times in his gospel, Mark has Jesus avoiding or outright rejecting, any reference to, or acclamation of being the Messiah. Initially, Matthew and Luke convey similar episodes in their gospels, but by the end of their respective narratives, it seems that Matthew and Luke have moved from the possibility of Jesus being the Messiah to the probability that he is the one sent from God as Jesus. More, the Jesus in Matthew and Luke's gospel has moved from being timid in regards to his divinity to one being ready to talk about it. Most confident among the later gospel writers that Jesus is positively God is John, and he the contents of his gospel prove it. If Jesus is not displaying his omnipotence by raising the dead, he is proclaiming his prestige by declaring he is the bread of life and the light of the world. According to the perspective of the later gospel writers, Jesus has gone from probable Messiah to possible Savior to positively God, and it's in this last manifestation that he will remain for the ages.

In all ways, one could rightly call the work of these gospel writers as indeed a work of art. Acting in retrospect, and artfully combining words, phrases, and even familiar places, the gospels are so expertly written to display Jesus' acts of teaching, display of miracles, and a new approach to ethics and morals that the writings became the theological standard the moment they began to circulate.

> *...if the contradictions, discrepancies, and inconsistencies in the later gospels provide enough conflict of evidence...to throw out the baby with the bathwater.*

Nevertheless, one must ask if the contradictions, discrepancies, and inconsistencies in the later gospels provide enough conflict of evidence regarding the birth, life, death, and resurrection of Jesus that we throw out the baby with the bathwater. Are the efforts of Matthew, Luke, and John to advance an individualistic narrative so deliberate and blatant that we must disregard everything these writers record in the gospels? More, do the specific labors of the later gospel writers to transform the historical Jesus into the Risen Christ unknowingly move Christians further and further away from the actual teachings of Jesus such that more attention is focused on the Messiah than the man called Jesus...more on the messenger than his message? Have the endeavors of Matthew, Luke, and John to show all the sides of Jesus, human and divine, weakened not only the argument of these three gospel writers but also create confusion and upheaval among the three texts? The more, the merrier, not so. The more, the muddier! One may even go as far as to speculate that these same three writers have possibly done lasting harm to the credibility of the ethical and moral lessons of Jesus as a whole by their intentional efforts. And all this happened because of different perspectives and different theologies. Undoubtedly, the later gospel writers intended to layout for individuals a road map of how they were to live their lives as devoted followers of Jesus by loving neighbor as self while challenging individuals to challenge culture and morals. The later gospel writers attempted to make their words action-based. But in the end, the

> ...*the approach must be a systematic one.*

differences and discrepancies in the narrative did little to point the way. With such a deep grained understanding of Jesus and the events surrounding his ministry, the task to separate wheat from the chaff will not be an easy one.

Joyously, a renaissance of the Christian faith is within reach, but only if Christians get back to the original, pure, and untainted teachings of Jesus, the man, and not the Christ as found in the gospels of the Matthew, Luke, and John. More, the approach must be a systematic one.

First, we must refrain from removing texts from their context. Just as a sentence helps to understand the meaning of a word or phrase within the sentence, the paragraph aids in understanding the sentence. Similarly, the chapter brings clarity to the paragraph, and so on. When a sentence is separated from the surrounding sentences, there is a good chance that the flow of that paragraph will be lost, because meaning commonly flows from larger units to smaller units and vice-versa. Further, the removal of a sentence from its surroundings emphasizes the particular sentence and not the larger thought. The same stands true regarding the removal of a specific verse from the passages that surround it. When a verse is separated from the adjoining verses, there is a chance that the meaning of that verse will either be misinterpreted or altogether lost. The scriptures are full of wisdom, but that wisdom is often misquoted and misunderstood when the text becomes detached from the surrounding texts. There is little wrong with applying a particular verse with a specific situation. Still,

> ...*refrain from manipulating the text.*

Backfill

it's essential to know what the verse was initially thought to convey. The discrepancies and inconsistencies of the scriptures, especially those found in the gospels, are better managed when one looks beyond the trees to the forest.

In like manner, we must refrain from manipulating the text. In this time of political and religious differences, the manipulation of the scriptures to fit a wide range of viewpoints is common. Instead of allowing the words of Jesus to shape our thoughts and actions, we in contemporary society have done just the opposite. We have seemingly not only highjacked the Jesus found in the gospels, but we have so bent and twisted his words that we have created our own narrative of the gospels. By manipulating and reconstructing the teachings of Jesus, it seems as though we have placed our words on his lips! More, it seems we have taken the wise and astute lessons of a first-century man and manipulated those words to fit into most any twenty-first-century situation. Consequently, it could be said that we are no better than those later gospel writers who not only reinvented the historical Jesus to fit a budding Christology but were equally successful in transforming him into the Risen Christ by a calculated manipulation of the events in his life. To avoid such a pitfall, we must make a concerted effort to have Jesus speak to and through us and not have it seem as though he is speaking for us.

Thirdly, we must keep an eye out for brackets around words and paragraphs in the scriptures, because they are there for a reason, as are footnotes. Brackets commonly indicate that a word, sentence, or paragraph is not in an earlier version of the text. The brackets around John 7:53-8:11 convey that the story was most likely not part of an earlier text. A writer somewhere along the way seems to have unilaterally decided to add the story of the adulterous woman to John's gospel. The same stands true for those teeny, tiny letters one commonly finds among the words of scripture. Those small letters refer to a note at the bottom of the page that provides us a little more information about a passage, person, or event. By taking note of these brackets, we can determine if the inclusion of the passage was a later one, or could have possibly been left out without affecting the content or the meaning of the writing?

> *...willing to follow the lead of Mathew, Luke, and John and rehabilitate and even reconstruct our Christology.*

Next, we must ask ourselves if we are willing to follow the lead of Matthew, Luke, and John and rehabilitate and even reconstruct our Christology. As shown, the later gospel writers were directly involved in developing a new understanding of an evolving Christ. It was Matthew who first began to backfill the events surrounding the life of Jesus using Mark's gospel as a foundation. By frontloading the genealogy of Jesus to his narrative, Matthew introduced added insight and understanding to the life of Jesus. However, Matthew did not stop there. By including additional events such as Jesus' Sermon on the Mount and more detail regarding the resurrection, Matthew can supply his readers with valuable information on this "evolving" Christ. The same could be said for Luke's gospel because it adds even more to the supposed specifics encompassing the birth, life, teaching, death, and resurrection of Jesus. By the time John's gospel appears in the late first century or early second century, the transformation of Jesus to Christ is complete. More, it's evident that the transformation of Jesus from man to Messiah by the later gospel writers was as much a spiritual reconstruction by the writers themselves as it was an effort by these same writers to communicate the transformation of Jesus to the world. Subsequently, the example of Matthew, Luke, and John to release themselves from traditionally held views of Jesus should stand to today's Christians as evidence of the value of a rehabilitated and reconstructed Christology.

Backfill

In closing, let me say that it has not been my goal in writing this book to take anything away from the gospel writers, especially the later ones we know as Matthew, Luke, and John. Little did they know that what they were writing would eventually be considered as sacred words. These writers were simply writing down episodes in the life of Jesus that they had heard from others. Furthermore, it's not as if these same writers were inventing anything about Jesus or even intentionally including about him at first. It was only after other writings began to appear that the inconsistencies and discrepancies came to light. So, can we rightfully blame them for what they wrote...absolutely not! There was basically one story of Jesus...the historical one...and then came his resurrection, and that changed everything. That singular event was enough to send the gospel writers to pen and paper

> *Capitalizing on the elements of chronology/time, context, and cause, along with backfilling the Jesus narrative as they went, these same gospel writers were successful...*

and the later gospel writers to reconstruct the life of an individual that had taken place five to ten decades earlier. Seeing this opportunity to both share the life of Jesus, and at the same time, including their understanding of the narrative of his life, the later gospel took it upon themselves to modify and reconstruct the story of Jesus. Capitalizing on the elements of chronology/time, context, and cause, along with backfilling the Jesus narrative as they went, these same writers were successful in demonstrating that the man from Nazareth indeed was God incarnate.

Likewise, it has not been my place to shine a not-so-positive light on the gospels of Matthew, Luke, or John. The pivotal work these three writers played, and continue to play, in shaping a set of beliefs that will continue long past most

Michael F. Price

who are reading this book will have breath. The means and the methods these three writers employed as they went about backfilling the Jesus narrative, starting on the perimeter of Jesus's life and working inward, utilizing as much of Mark's content as they saw fit, using small pieces of material to create a more compact backfill, packing the material, and finally, blending in their specific content, can rightfully be considered a real work of art.

Instead, my intent in writing this book is to open a conversation that centers on how Christians are to deal with the contradictions, inconsistencies, and discrepancies that are found in the writings of these later gospel writers since these issues possess the potential to distract us as we study the scriptures. Try as we may, these issues cannot be overlooked. The best we can do is to not only validate them but work through them as we seek to align our words and our ways with those of Jesus.

Dr. Michael F. Price
Largo, FL

www.ingramcontent.com/pod-product-compliance
Lightning Source LLC
Chambersburg PA
CBHW070853050426
42453CB00012B/2171